Vital Business Secrets for New and Growing Companies

Vital Business Secrets for New and Growing Companies

L. Joseph Schmoke
Richard R. Allen

Dow Jones-Irwin
Homewood, Illinois 60430

124969

Sponsoring editor: Jim Childs
Project editor: Joan Hopkins
Production manager: Carma W. Fazio
Jacket designer: Sam Concialdi
Compositor: Publication Services, Inc.
Typeface: 11/13 Century Schoolbook
Printer: Arcata Graphics/Kingsport

LIBRARY OF CONGRESS
Library of Congress Cataloging-in-Publication Data

Schmoke, L. Joseph.
      Vital business secrets for new and growing companies / L. Joseph
Schmoke, Richard R. Allen
          p.   cm.
      Includes index.
      ISBN 1-556-23124-5
      1. New business enterprises.   2. Success in business.   I. Allen,
Richard R., 1952-   . II. Title.
HD62.5.S353 1989
658—dc19   88–21762
                                                                                        CIP

Printed in the United States of America
1 2 3 4 5 6 7 8 9 0 K 5 4 3 2 1 0 9 8

To Diana
and
To Kathleen

INTRODUCTION

Why is it that some businesses soar to success, while others seem destined to fail despite viable products and diligent efforts by owners and managers? Many of the businesspeople behind those failures seem to know their industry or speciality extremely well. What is it that sets them apart from their successful counterparts? Something seems to be missing—some critical piece of the "puzzle" that, if found, would make everything fit into place. What is this missing piece?

The missing piece that makes a business successful is often an understanding of business strategies, techniques, and insights that can take years to learn. Frequently, these insights are protected by those who have learned them, shrouded by an aura of mystery and sophistication. These are the secrets of business, and they can bring success and growth to a company, whether it is a startup or an established firm.

This book has been written to present those secrets to you—this inside information—and to help you solve the many puzzles of starting and running a business. Applying these secrets will give you an edge in today's business environment, a highly competitive environment that sees nearly 80 percent of new businesses fail within their first five years. Our aim is to help you triumph over the odds, so that you don't become one of these well-publicized entrepreneurial casualties. By arming yourself with the information in this book, you can firmly establish your business, increase your profits, and eventually position yourself for the acquisition of other companies, for a profitable sale to another company, or for an Initial Public Offering (IPO).

WHO CAN BENEFIT BY READING THIS BOOK

Anyone who is currently operating a business, whether its revenues are $100,000 or $50,000,000 per year, will find the information in this book indispensable. Twenty years of experience with building, running, and financing profitable businesses will be at your fingertips.

Those who are thinking of starting their very first business will be taken, step-by-step, through the process of a startup. We understand the questions and concerns that arise when a business is begun, and we answer those questions and address those concerns. We show you in clear terms how to transform your thoughts and ideas into the reality of your own business.

Rising managers in mid-size companies will affirm that the straightforward and unique wisdom contained in this book offers insight into proven, practical secrets that otherwise might take years to learn. The rise to the top will be helped by the techniques and strategies found in these chapters.

The professionals of the business world also can use the information we've packed into these pages. Whether you are an attorney, an accountant, an investment banker, commercial lender, or other service professional, you will be able to broaden your knowledge and understanding in many areas: successful startup planning, raising money for a business, the acquisition process, initial public offerings, business plan creation, and other essential keys to business success. This specialized knowledge will help you to attract and service new clients.

Students will find that the insights and methods presented in these chapters are much more substantial than the sometimes untested theories of the academic world. You will find that the messages and information contained here are timeless and can be called up on demand for years to come.

A NEW PERSPECTIVE

Regardless of your level of business experience—whether you are just starting out or whether you are a seasoned pro— this book offers new perspectives on common problems. Our approaches are sometimes unconventional, but always concise, understandable, and genuinely usable.

We include answers to difficult questions such as the amount of equity that should be given up to investors, a secret that, alone, is worth the price of the book.

This book gives you everything from the basics of creating a startup and financing it, to acquiring an existing business, to building a company through policies leading to controlled but steady growth.

Methods and sources for research are given; these are invaluable in the evaluation of your prospective business, your competitors, and possible acquisition candidates.

Negotiating techniques for closing deals are covered in great depth. These show you how you can become adept at dealing with attorneys, accountants, and investment bankers, so that your relations with these professionals are not one-sided in their favor. Methods for keeping your business profitable and efficient are also revealed.

The world of business is a fascinating and stimulating one. Its rewards can be great in terms of both monetary gain and personal achievement. Statistics show that real business success is often difficult to accomplish, but you can improve your chances considerably by following the advice offered in these pages.

We hope you enjoy the book, that you find yourself mentally stimulated and encouraged by it, and that you use it successfully for many years to come.

L. Joseph Schmoke
Richard R. Allen

CONTENTS

CHAPTER 1

THE SUCCESSFUL STARTUP

It's easy to start a business. It isn't easy to start the right *business the* right *way.*

In This Chapter:

1. Commitment is critical
2. Choosing the right business or industry
3. Basic business survival skills
4. Researching your choices
5. Which business is best? A test

GETTING STARTED

Thousands of new businesses are begun every year, so obviously it isn't too difficult to embark on a new venture. But as many as 80 percent—the vast majority—of these startups are out of business within three to five years. Why? Although it is relatively easy to start a business, it is quite difficult to choose the right business and to go about the process of a startup in a manner that will lead to success. For many entrepreneurs and businesspeople it takes two or three tries before they learn all the critical steps in the startup process; some never learn.

The specific steps, the techniques, and the psychological advantages that are revealed to you in this chapter, coupled with the insights and guidance in the following chapters, will be indispensable if you want to succeed. The survival of your startup may well depend of the inside information you garner from these pages. And your continued success and prosperity will most certainly be enhanced by the application of these principles.

COMMITMENT IS CRITICAL

We are acquainted with an individual who has recently completed his third startup. His first was in the health club business, where he created a multiple-location operation featuring racquetball courts. He was perceptive enough to have recognized an early trend toward racquetball, but his perception and luck later became a liability. He had been so successful, so easily, early in his business career that when the saturation point arrived in the racquetball market, he was taken by surprise. He thought his work had ended once the startup phase ended. This led to the demise of his health club business.

This individual then started a chain of restaurants in the pizza parlor industry. The problem encountered this time was a lack of personal commitment. Since there were multiple partners involved in this venture, all felt they could expend proportionately less effort than if they had been alone in the venture. The result was that the first of many planned restaurants opened almost a year behind schedule. This threw the other planned openings off schedule, and before they had a chance to establish themselves in their targeted geographic areas, the pizza segment of the restaurant market had become saturated. Their opportunity had passed them by.

Eleven years had passed since the first startup, and this businessman had learned some hard, costly lessons. Now he was battle-scarred but experienced, and he was ready to go back into business. But this time he vowed to do everything the best way he possibly could. Nothing would stand in the way of success. He made a rigid commitment to properly prepare for his new venture, a real estate development. The planning process, which included a thorough and objective study of various markets, took over a year.

Market studies indicated that specific areas of Florida were ideal for mid-sized shopping centers, and the businessman moved his family of four over 1200 miles to be in the right place.

The time involved in his preparation, and the objectivity with which he did his research and planning, demonstrated his level of commitment. He had learned—the hard way—that a strong commitment was a necessary step in the creation of a strong start up. Today, this businessman is a successful commercial developer in southwest Florida.

Before taking any action toward starting a business, it is vital that you understand the tremendous mental and emotional commitment that will be required of you. If your startup is being done by a team of founders, then it is essential that each founder make this commitment.

The *mental* commitment is a dedication to follow all the steps that lead to the creation of a business in the best possible manner: in a word, *discipline*—no shortcuts, no skipping a step or two, but 100 percent commitment to following the correct formula.

The *emotional* commitment you must make may seem to come more naturally, but it is no less essential: You must have the passion to see your startup through all its phases, to devote tremendous amounts of time and energy to properly gathering all the facts and information you need to make the right decisions.

The reason we like to discuss these two commitments as being separate and distinct is that they may, at some point, come into conflict with one another. If they do, it's important for you to know which to follow.

There may come a time when, after having spent months on your startup process, the facts and information you have obtained make it seem that the potential rewards from your venture may not be worth the risks involved. Up to that point, your emotional commitment has given you the drive and determination to gather and cull all this information. But it is your mental commitment that will help you make your "go" or "no-go" decision, where you must decide to forge ahead or call it quits.

You will have to be coldly rational and put all your emotions aside to make this decision. Forgetting all the time and energy you have invested, you will have to look at what your information is telling you and listen to your common sense. Remember, **there is no right way to do the wrong thing.**

The Importance of Discipline

Discipline is probably the most important attribute needed for successful completion of the startup process. And it will remain important even when the business is up and running.   You must discipline yourself to do the things necessary to get your business off the ground.   Then you must discipline yourself to pay attention to all the details of operating your business so that it doesn't return to the ground with a deafening crash. No one is going to force you to do what we tell you to do in this book, and no one is going to be looking over your shoulder to see if you've covered all the bases. It's entirely up to you.

After reading this book, you'll know what steps to take and how to take them.   But without self-discipline you'll have a hard time making much headway, and you'll have problems keeping your business running in an efficient and profitable manner.

Full-Time Commitment

The distractions of daily life are enough of a burden for most people. But a computer engineer with whom we're acquainted (we'll call him Ed) wanted to add to his burden by starting his own business in specialty radio paging. He had a wife and small children, a house, and a full-time job with a major electronics firm.

Ed talked about his startup with anyone who would listen, and finally was referred to investors who were capable of funding his new venture. But Ed had not taken the time to prepare a business plan. Nor did he have a prototype product. Nor had he gathered any market research. All Ed had was an idea, and this just wasn't enough for these experienced investors.

Two years passed before Ed fashioned a business plan, at which time he approached the investors again.   He still had no prototype, no market studies. When the investors asked Ed why it had taken him so long to provide them with a business plan, and why he didn't have a prototype or market research, he explained that he had "been too busy" between work and caring for the children.

To the investors, Ed was saying, "I am really doing this as

a hobby, not as a business." If he had been serious about the business prospects for his idea, he would have approached the project in a more disciplined manner. The investors realized that it takes a disciplined individual to run a successful company, and they didn't want to bet on someone who would be easily distracted. Such a lack of commitment is a warning flag to any experienced investor.

Needless to say, Ed did not get the funding he was seeking. But he is still talking to anyone who will listen. After all, one has to have a hobby.

Startups Are Time Consuming

While the startup process may not cost a lot of money, it will certainly take a lot of time. And it has to be *your* time. Of course, you can hire professionals to guide you through your startup, but the good ones will insist that they act only as *guides*. Having a consultant or other professional do most of the legwork for your startup will end up being a disadvantage and will reduce your chance of success.

There is no substitute for having a thorough and detailed knowledge of your proposed business: knowledge of your industry, knowledge of your competitors and the marketplace in which you must compete, and intimate knowledge of the concept, service, or product you plan to provide. You will live with the results of these efforts for a long time, while the consultants you use will take on other clients and fade from the scene. It will take time to learn the intricacies of your business and to design the strategies that will make it successful, profitable, and long-lasting. And you must be committed to investing that time.

CHOOSING THE RIGHT BUSINESS OR INDUSTRY

Let's assume that you aren't certain which type of business you want to enter. Obviously, this assumption isn't valid for everyone, as some of us have always wanted to enter one type of business or another. But it's wise for everyone to mentally go through the steps suggested here, just to be sure all the significant factors have been considered in this most important decision.

A Key Consideration: Personal Objectives

The first thing that enters the minds of many would-be entrepreneurs when they consider the type of business they want to enter is "What can I do to make a lot of money?" Whatever type of business seems the most profitable is the one they want to start.

While making money is an important consideration, it is not the only criterion, nor the most important one, for selecting your area of business. You should realize that if you end up in a business you don't really like, you probably won't make much money

A new business requires a tremendous amount of energy, and it's hard to sustain that energy if you aren't happy with what you're doing. Also be aware that the profitability of your business venture will very likely be tied directly to your knowledge and experience. The decision regarding which type of business is best for you is one that requires thought, research, soul-searching, and honest objectivity.

The business you enter should satisfy your *personal objectives*. What are these personal objectives? They are the goals and priorities that are important to *you*, and they need to be written down and analyzed before you make another move.

• What kind of lifestyle do you want? Do you want and need fancy cars, world travel, custom-made clothes, private schools for your children, and the like? Or do you prefer a more conservative lifestyle, without the image of wealth?
• Where do you want to live? Is the climate important? Do you want mountains or the sea? Do you like a medium-sized town, or do you prefer the cultural diversity of a large city? As long as you're considering change, you might as well live where you will be most happy.
• How hard do you want to work? You may have an unlimited amount of time to devote to your business, or you may want to limit yourself to 10 hours a week. Whatever you want is all

right, but your choices are going to be very limited if your time is too.

• What size company do you want to run? Perhaps you would like the challenge of directing 1000 employees and 20 different branch offices, or maybe you don't care much for the friction that can come from working with dozens of subordinates. Obviously, there aren't very many one- or two-person businesses that can generate six figure salaries for their owners. Your desires for income and lifestyle should not be at odds with the size of the business you want to run. If they are, you'll have to change one for the other or compromise a little.

• What are your spouse's desires? This business is going to affect your wife or husband just as much as it will you. And you need all the support you can get. It's certainly better to have an ally at home than an enemy.

A Comment for Married Entrepreneurs

This point warrants more than just a passing reference. It is extremely important that you gain the moral support of your family *before* you begin the process of starting your business. You need every advantage available in starting a business endeavor, and you would certainly be putting yourself at a *disadvantage* if you did not have the strong support of your spouse.

Running your own business takes quite a toll on your personal life—it's nearly impossible not to take the business home with you—and having your husband or wife on your side can be the thing that makes it work for you. So bring your spouse into the planning stage with you, from this very moment. If you're successful, your spouse will share in the rewards with you. If you're not successful, your spouse will help you face the consequences.

Which Business Best Suits You?

A client with whom we've worked closely for over 15 years had been very successful in specialty retailing. He had also developed a rapidly growing subsidiary in wholesale distribution.

Both these businesses were in the same industry, and the client knew that industry well.

An opportunity presented itself that would allow the businessman to diversify into the manufacturing of items for the recreational vehicle market. The businessman was convinced that his success in running two businesses indicated an aptitude for running *any* business. After all, he thought, wasn't this new business driven by the same demand for new and unique products which drove the other two?

Unfortunately, the answer was not what he had expected. The businessman quickly found that new skills and discipline were required by the manufacturing business. Inventory control had to be matched to both orders and a production schedule. Productivity had to be measured, and quality control had to be monitored. All these skills were foreign to our client, and it took him over a year to realize that he did not have the slightest idea of what was going on in his 12,000 square foot production facility. He was, however, smart enough to know that he had a negative cash flow that was getting larger every month. *That* was something he could understand.

The new company was eventually liquidated, with our businessman being far and away the biggest creditor. He constantly refers to the experience as being the most expensive graduate course in business he ever took. And all he learned was what might seem like common sense (but what is often ignored): "Do what you do best."

Match Skills to the Industry

The next step in your planning process, then, is a very important one: to choose a particular industry or business that suits you well. The business needs to be one in which you can apply your own special skills and experience. While this may sound like too basic a first step, it isn't as easy as you might suppose.

First, make an assessment of your skills and experience, and then decide what you do best. Many industries or businesses require special skills or knowledge for successful operation, and the skills from one type of job may not be transferable to another. Just because someone is successful as a retailer, for example, doesn't mean she will be successful as a manufacturer. Even though branching into manufacturing would theoretically reduce the retailer's cost of merchandise, the risk of entering a business that demands skills foreign to the retailer might be too high to justify that diversification. Skills in sales, marketing, purchasing, and advertising are of little help in the world of manufacturing, with its emphasis on inventory levels, batch-work production, and factory overhead controls.

Some people are good at making things, some at selling them, and others at designing them. Don't try to do what you're *not* experienced at, just because it seems more glamorous, appears more exciting, or seems to offer more profit.

In assessing your abilities, be brutally honest. Take an actual "skill inventory." What have you done in your life that you are particularly good at? What do you *like* to do? Are you familiar with financial statements or with borrowing procedures? Are you good with people, hiring the right ones, and managing them well? Can you fire people when the situation calls for it? Where do your shortcomings lie? *Be honest*: You know you have shortcomings—all of us do. Can you overcome them or work around them?

It isn't necessary, or even desirable, for you to master all the skills needed to run a particular type of business, but it *is* necessary for you to know the areas where you need help. You must be able to assume the role of leader, organizer, and coordinator if you plan on building your business beyond a one- or two-person operation. Some of the skills you need can be learned, but only if you're able to identify the ones you *need* to learn.

Identify Your Personal Skills and Experience

Produce a skill and experience inventory for yourself by answering the following questions.

1. What jobs have you held in your adult life? Include self-employment.
2. What duties and responsibilities did you have on these jobs? List these separately.
3. Which of these duties have you handled particularly well? Which have you *not* performed so well? Which

duties have you most enjoyed, even if you weren't particularly good at them? Make three separate lists of these
duties.

4. What aptitude do you have for numbers? Do you know
   how to record your own financial transactions?
5. How well do you interact with people? Are you a leader
   and a motivator?
6. Have you ever sold anything? Can you? Or does selling
   intimidate you?

BASIC BUSINESS SURVIVAL SKILLS

Once you've completed your personal skill and experience
inventory, you should compare your skills with those necessary
to successfully operate a business. We call these the *basic survival skills* of business.

1. Basic Record Keeping Skills—The ability to produce the
   records necessary to track your company's performance.
2. Financial Management Skills—The ability to understand the information produced by the record keeping
   system and apply it to the day-to-day operations of the
   company, to best utilize the company's resources.
3. Personnel Management Skills—The ability to hire, fire,
   train, and supervise employees, and to delegate responsibilities to these employees.
4. Marketing Skills—The ability to identify your customer
   base and determine the most effective means of convincing them to buy.
5. Knowledge of Your Product or Service—A thorough and
   complete knowledge of what you have to offer.
6. Communication Skills—The ability to clearly explain
   your ideas, and to produce a desired response in people.

It's very doubtful that you have *all* these skills, and it's
important for you to decide which ones could use improvement.
Your choices are either to learn them before you get started, to
hire someone else who already possesses them, or to "wing it"
without them and learn them as you go. We do not recommend

the latter. Even successful businesspeople sometimes venture into areas where they have no experience or expertise, and many encounter failure when they do. Identify what it is that you do best and stick with it—at least until you can afford to risk failure.

Corporate Aptitude and Experience

Just like individuals, no company possesses an aptitude for every type of business. Even the largest international conglomerates find they can lose money when they tackle areas in which they have no experience. So it is necessary to objectively determine the specific skills your company possesses; not what you would *like* your company to be, but what it *is*.

What Is Done to Create Revenue?
Step one is to identify the different processes that exist in your "core" business. For example, do you buy raw material, make a finished product out of it, package it, and then ship it to your customers? Or do you buy finished products that are already packaged, display them in a store, advertise the store and/or the products, and then sell them to a customer who comes to your place of business?

The key is to identify the steps that are taken to generate revenues. These steps will be unique for each business, and it just takes common sense to identify the phases that products move through on the way to becoming sales.

What Is Performed Best by the Company?
Step two is to rank the processes you identify in step one according to how well your company performs each process. Using the input of all the departments within your company, number the processes from the best to the worst, with a brief explanation of your reasons for the ranking. To help you with your decisions, assume that your company could perform only one or two of the processes. Which one or two would you choose? Which can you do most profitably? Which would you be quickest to eliminate? These rankings will help to uncover specific skills that could be used in a different business or industry.

Who Are the Company's Customers?

Try to identify your market by clear-cut customer profiles. As an example, a company in the building products industry might be able to classify its major buyers as (1) retail home improvement stores, (2) lumber yards, (3) regional and national retailers (such as Sears and K mart), or (4) large national home builders. List the major buyer/customer profiles for *your* company.

What Else Can the Company Sell?

Now examine the list of customer groups to find those with whom you have a special rapport or relationship. What other goods and services do these groups presently buy? What others might they consider buying in the future? Are there any of these other goods and services that *your* company might be able to provide, using the same general processes you listed as your "best" in step two?

The objective here is to think of new ways to utilize both the best of your customer base and your company's most profitable processes. Our sample building products company might have found that its best process was its ability to take a material (wood), finish it to a sanded stage, and deliver it in bulk quantities to retail centers, and that its best relationships were with the big national chains.

How could these skills be translated into another profitable business? Perhaps by taking the cutting and finishing process one step further and getting into the unfinished furniture business, using the national chains for the retailing. Once the strengths of your market and production processes have been identified, brainstorming becomes much easier, much more focused, and effective.

Rank Potential Businesses

Now that you've gone through the preceding steps of listing personal objectives and ranking your personal or corporate skills and experience, you'll find you've stimulated some new ideas and developed a better focus. Now is the time to narrow your potential choices down to a few industries or businesses that best suit your circumstances and abilities. The first step is make two lists.

1. List the businesses you'd like to be in. Take a few minutes to rank the businesses you've chosen by their appeal to you. At this point, the *reason* a business appeals to you is not really important. It could be because of the glamour involved with it, or because it seems the most potentially lucrative. Whatever the reason, rank the businesses on a scale from 1 to 10.

2. List the businesses you're *qualified* to be in. By now you've given some serious thought to your skills and experience. Use this thought to rank the businesses you've selected according to how well you could perform in each venture.

Take the two lists of businesses and compare them. If there are more than eight or ten entries in total, eliminate those with the lowest rankings. Consolidate the lists to include only those entries that appear in both places, and get ready to do some time-consuming research on these candidates.

A Pointer on Narrowing the Field

Sometimes it can be pretty difficult to narrow the choice of business possibilities down to a reasonable number. Everything looks good! If this difficulty occurs, try approaching the task in reverse: Eliminate those businesses in which you definitely do not want to be involved. If you hate getting your hands dirty, eliminate auto repair, landscaping, and anything else that might entail even occasional manual labor. If you have no appreciation for mechanical or electrical contrivances, eliminate anything that deals with them.

The object here is to "take a swipe" at the things you dislike and, in so doing, get the creative juices flowing a bit. By the time you're through, you'll find that it's suddenly easier for you to think of businesses that are legitimate possibilities, and you'll better understand *why* some of those businesses appeal to you.

RESEARCHING YOUR CHOICES

After going through these mental exercises and spending the time to come up with several intelligent choices of businesses, you will have reached the examination stage. Give each of these choices some subjective and objective examination. You'll find while doing this that you will learn a lot about both the industry you have chosen and the market in which you will compete. By the time you have completed a thorough analysis of each of your choices, you will have gained important insights into each of these businesses, and these insights will help you to make your final decision as to which is most right for you.

A Suggestion on Notetaking

Always *date* the notes you take, and include the *source* and *location* of the material you've used. The information you gather will be invaluable to you in later stages of your startup, when you've selected one particular industry on which to focus your energies. Such references to sources of facts and figures can be included in your business plan, or in any presentation to investors or lenders, and will greatly enhance your credibility with them.

RESEARCH: WHERE TO LOOK

One of the *most important things* that you will learn from this book is where to go to find detailed business information which, if you had to pay for it, would be worth thousands of dollars. The authors have found, to their amazement, that virtual treasure troves of business information are available simply for the asking. Once you learn the secrets of *where to look* and *what to look for*, you will find that your use of this tool will continue for as long as you are in business.

The Ideal Data Source

In the utopia of business research, you would have access to all the information published about economic trends and forecasts, business and industry trends, performance and analysis, and detailed information on the leading companies in any specific industry. The volumes would fill large rooms, and would occupy reels of microfilm and computer disks. This reference library would cost a fortune to build and another to maintain, as the best and most timely information should be updated constantly to be most useful.

The Library Reference Section

This ideal reference library actually exists, and it is available for your use whenever you choose to use it, at little or no charge. It is the *Reference Section* of the major library nearest your home or office. We use the term *major library* because you won't find a complete reference section in most neighborhood branch libraries, or in many small-town libraries. The best libraries for this type of research are those located at colleges and universities, and the main library in any major city in the country.

The big difference between college libraries and public ones is that school libraries often restrict your ability to borrow books if you are not affiliated with the school. Fortunately, this is of little importance to you, for the type of research you will be doing involves reference books that can't normally be checked out of public libraries either.

The authors have found, without exception, that they are always welcomed (and never questioned) at the college libraries that they have used for research across the country. Don't be shy about using these facilities—that's why they're there. Just use common sense and courtesy and follow all the library's rules, and you will always be welcome.

As obvious as this may sound, you should *use the librarian assigned to the reference section!* You will be amazed at the skill and knowledge of this person, who will be able to quickly guide you to exactly what you are searching for, and may even find additional information you would not have thought to ask for in the first place.

There are many books, directories, and reports in the reference section that you may find helpful, and we can't begin to list them all, but several specific reference works are always useful. We have listed these works in Appendix C, where we briefly explain their contents and how to use them.

Other Sources of Information

In addition to the materials found in the reference section and periodical room of a major library, there are several other sources of information you can use for researching potential businesses. For those who have personal computers, a relatively new and potentially valuable source of business information has been developed in the new *database services*. By using these services you can search for information on literally millions of companies, conducting your search by specific industry or product, or by specific topics.

As an example, a search for "Toxic Waste—Cleanup," for all companies with sales between $1 million and $5 million annually, would produce a list of all the companies of this size that are involved in toxic waste cleanup. From those companies, some could be selected for more detailed financial information and reports.

Dun & Bradstreet was one of the original firms to offer traditional financial information via the computer, and is still one of the largest, but many others have entered the arena offering other types of business information. You can learn more about these services by requesting information from the various companies advertising in business and financial magazines.

A more traditional source of business information is the stock brokerage firms, which publish research reports on various industries as well as on individual companies. These reports are usually available for the asking through the larger firms.

You may also want to attend conventions and meetings held by various industry and trade associations. You can learn of these by reading the trade magazines and newspapers found in the periodical section of the library. And you can always do a little of your own detective work to find information sources we haven't mentioned here.

The Five Essential Decision Factors

These reference and resource materials will present you with a massive amount of information, much of which may not be of immediate use but may be useful to you in the future. For now, though, you need to sort through this material to gain some new insights into the industry or business you're considering. Your goal is to confirm that an industry is a good one to be in, or to discover why it doesn't offer the opportunities you believed it did. To reach this evaluation stage, look for the following five decision factors in the information you've uncovered.

Trends

After reading the various assessments the experts have given of an industry or business, a definite trend will usually be clear. It may be that the industry is entering a phase of rapid expansion that is expected to last for a period of months or years. Or the reverse might be the case, where all indications are pointing to slow growth. This may indicate that it would be a poor time to enter the industry, or it might present an opportunity for you to try some new concepts for a product or service. Whatever the trends mean to you, it's important that they be spotted *before* you become involved in the industry.

Predictions and Projections

Industry reports and forecasts offer various predictions for the future in both general and very specific terms. You may agree or disagree with these professionals' conclusions—they are not always correct—but they supply another viewpoint, an educated one, concerning the economy and the industry you are studying. If your concept of future trends is in agreement with the experts, you will at least know that your conclusions are supported by others. If, however, you feel you are very much alone in your predictions, then you should take a step back and rethink your position.

Potential investors will learn through their own sources (if they don't already know) that you are about to make a strategic mistake by bucking an obvious trend. They will either withdraw their support or ask you to convince them that you are right, even though the general consensus weighs against you. All things considered, it's very difficult to do the latter.

Cyclical or Seasonal Characteristics

Cyclical refers to broad economic cycles, which may last several years, whereas *seasonal* refers to a recurring annual change such as spring or winter. There are few industries that are not affected in one way or another by economic cycles (we can't think of any). A retail toy store is obviously seasonal in that the bulk of its business is done during the Christmas season. A company that produces pleasure boats may be both seasonal and cyclical: Its boats may not sell well during an economic recession, but even when the economy is strong the boats may not sell as well during the winter months as during the summer.

By reading the research material, you should be able to learn if the industry you are considering entering is affected by seasonal or cyclical factors. Look at quarterly sales and profits for publicly held companies, and consider the economic reports from the Department of Commerce and Standard & Poor's and what the trade publications have to say.

Dominant Companies

Each industry has its dominant companies—its leaders and innovators—and these companies often have a great effect on the industry as a whole. You can learn a lot from these companies: strategy, tactics, assessments of what the future holds, new markets to approach, and many other things. You may also learn that these leading companies have so completely dominated the market that there is no niche left for you. Or you may learn that they have missed some need that you can fill, signaling an opportunity for you.

The dominant companies in most industries are likely to be publicly held, and you can obtain their addresses and phone numbers from the Dun & Bradstreet or Standard & Poor's Directories. Write to the companies and ask for their annual reports and 10-K's. Read these reports thoroughly and take notes on anything that might help you make your business decisions.

Average Financial Ratios

You will find that there are several sources for average financial performance ratios—ratios such as "return on sales," "return on equity," and "rate of growth." The industry reports written by the Department of Commerce and Standard & Poor's will include a wide range of financial averages obtained from companies within an industry. These averages will prove beneficial to you when you create your own financial forecasts, and will serve as a comparison guideline to ensure that your own numbers are not out of line with your industry's.

Professional investors use these averages to judge the accuracy of your projections and forecasts, and to determine whether your expectations are realistic. You should know in advance what your projections are going to be compared against, because it helps you keep those projections believable. Knowing these averages gives you an idea about what costs and profits can be expected from a mature company in a particular industry. Some of these financial ratios are presented in Appendix B.

Some Hints on Picking the Best Business for You

By persevering in researching the reference material we've suggested, several potential businesses will be eliminated in the process. Your research and common sense will make obvious which ones to reject and which warrant further investigation. A definite feeling will develop that one business is better for you than another.

One of our acquaintances had spent a number of years as a restaurant operator, and he'd been very successful at it. Eventually, though, he had tired of the long hours and the constant employee turnover, pilferage, and dependence on weather and other uncontrollable factors. But he really liked food and enjoyed interacting with people. He also needed an income sufficient to support his lifestyle.

The ex-restaurateur examined many food-related businesses, including such diverse enterprises as importing seafood from Central America, wholesaling meat and poultry to restaurants and hotels, and creating his own line of specialty foods. None of these really seemed satisfying, though. So he expanded his research even further. He read as many industry magazines as he could find. Finally, he found a concept that appealed to him.

Several of the articles he had read described the success of new specialty-food departments in supermarkets, especially those located in upscale areas. It was also apparent from many articles he had found that more and more people were willing to pay extra for quality. All the factors seemed to add up, and the businessman was convinced that a specialty gourmet grocery store could satisfy all his requirements.

After a year of fine-tuning, his gourmet grocery opened in the high-income area of a major city. He carried fine restaurant-grade prime meats, fresh fish, cut flowers, gourmet sauces and condiments, and a large selection of fine wines. Fresh bread, muffins, rolls, and pastries were baked on the premises, and there was a selection of fine coffees. It was as if his restaurant had metamorphosed into an intimate and personal retail store.

This man "knew" that his concept would be the perfect combination to satisfy all of his needs. He would be able to interact with customers, deal with food, wine, and other items that he knew so well, and make a good living while doing it. There was no specific formula he followed to reach his decision; he simply researched his choices until a satisfactory answer emerged. He was possessed with the "feeling" that this was the perfect business for him, and it was.

That feeling is important and it should be followed, as long as it doesn't conflict with your stated objectives (income, responsibility, lifestyle, experience, etc.). Discuss your selection with trusted and experienced advisors and solicit their opinions of your chances for success in a particular business. But don't rely solely on their advice. Your own instincts should always take precedence over third-party opinions.

WHICH BUSINESS IS REALLY BEST? A TEST

As a final test of which business is really the best for you, ask yourself these questions.

1. Does the product or service this business provides fill a real need? If so, how great is the need and how many competitors are attempting to fill it? Do these competitors have an insurmountable advantage over new entries in the business?

2. Is the business you've selected positioned in a fragile niche? Is it susceptible to rapid changes (technology, fashions, etc.) or might it be operating in a saturated market (such as fast-food restaurants)?

3. Is the business in a glamorous field that everyone else is rushing into? Or is it in a less popular field where little new competition can be expected?

4. Is the product or service you plan to offer a variation of something that already exists, or is it a new idea? If it's brand new, are you aware that the majority of pioneering efforts in the business world are long, costly, and frustrating affairs? Even IBM didn't enter the personal computer market until it had been developed by other companies, many of whom never survived long enough to see the market begin to mature.

5. Do you feel comfortable with the business and industry, based upon your personal experience, talent, and expectations?

If you can answer these final questions positively, it very likely means that you have settled on a business that is well-suited for *you*. This means that your first step will be the best one possible. Now, by applying everything you have learned from your research, and bringing the same level of commitment to the actual startup phase that you brought to the research, you will increase your chances of success manyfold in your chosen business.

CHAPTER 2

CREATING A DYNAMIC
BUSINESS STRATEGY

An essential roadmap to success

In This Chapter:

1. Seven reasons for preparing a business plan
2. Business plan—an outline, explained in great detail
3. An investor's viewpoint

TANGIBLE EVIDENCE OF YOUR
INTANGIBLE IDEAS

Now that you have completed the exploratory research stage, the next step in creating a business is to prepare a written business plan. Some may say, "I'm a smart person and I can keep track of everything in my head. Why write a business plan when I already know what to do?" There are many reasons why a business plan should be written, and some of those are enumerated below. But perhaps the best reason is that, by doing so, your business will gain a significant advantage over the competition.

SEVEN REASONS FOR PREPARING A BUSINESS PLAN

1. It is virtually impossible to raise money for a business without a business plan.

2. A business plan forces you to examine and consider each and every facet of your proposed venture, including the details which can make or break you in business.

3. Once you begin running a business, you will be constantly distracted by little details which are nonproductive. These distractions tend to obscure your original objectives, and a business can begin to drift without direction. A specific plan focuses your time and energy on the original business objectives.

4. Business is "doing battle" with the competition for the consumer dollar. Successful generals do not enter a war, or even a minor battle, without planning their strategy. A complete business plan is a clear, written strategy for winning a battle in the marketplace.

5. The "concept" for a business is an intangible thing. You can't see it or touch it, and neither can other people, such as investors, partners, or key employees. A written business plan is tangible evidence of your thoughts, concepts, and research. It can be seen, touched, and studied. The plan projects the notion that your business already exists. This is a tremendous psychological advantage.

6. A business plan tells people—investors, lenders, *you*— where you are going and how you intend to get there. It is your roadmap, and without it you might end up traveling in circles.

7. A business plan makes the difficult task of starting, running, and building a business much easier. Just ask those who have attempted startups both ways: They can attest to the value of this essential tool.

*In the creation of a business plan, the **most important** elements of a particular venture are isolated, researched, and weighed. From this work, a **detailed business strategy** is formulated **in writing**.* Over the years, we have developed a general outline which we use exclusively in writing business plans. This is the format we suggest you use for your enterprise. But before we deal with the physical appearance of the business plan, we will first turn our attention to the contents.

BUSINESS PLAN—AN OUTLINE

The business plan is broken down into approximately 12 distinct sections, each covering a specific topic in some detail. You may choose to eliminate, add, or combine some of the sections once you have read through and edited the entire plan.

The order in which the sections of the plan are written is not important, with one key exception: The Summary (or Executive Summary, as it is sometimes called) should be done last. The Summary contains all the highlights of the entire plan, and the author has a better concept of those highlights after the individual sections have been completed.

Always use Roman numerals to denote the different sections of the business plan, and then capital letters for each subsection under the main topic. The following is a standard format for a startup business plan.

Each section's contents are inclosed in a box (for this book's purposes only) and then explained in detail.

I. SUMMARY (or EXECUTIVE SUMMARY)

> I. Summary (or Executive Summary)
>   A. The Product (or Concept)—Present and Planned
>   B. The Market
>   C. Unique Features
>   D. Proposed Financing

Remember, this section should be written last, after the rest of the business plan has been completed.

The length of the Summary should not exceed two or three pages. It is not unusual to rewrite the Summary section several times before it takes on its final form. Spend the time and effort to make the Summary well-written and complete. It is the first section which will be read by prospective investors. If the Summary doesn't interest the reader, the plan will be quickly relegated to the reject pile.

A. The Product (or Concept)—Present and Planned

This subsection explains what will be offered to the potential market, both the products or services which will be immediately available, and future products that will be offered by the company. Keep your comments brief in this section. There is a full section later in the business plan where a detailed description will be given.

B. The Market

Describe potential customers: Who are they? Where are they? How are they identified? How do you plan to reach them? The basic question, "Who is going to buy from your company?" must be answered in this section. Again, as in all sections of the Summary, do not give a great deal of detail—just an overview of the market.

C. Unique Features

What makes your product or service stand apart from your competitors'? What special market niches are you addressing? What is proprietary about what you are offering? Answer these questions as concisely as possible.

D. Proposed Financing

Briefly address the financing required for your business and how you will use the funds. Include the terms of your offering, and specify the type of securities you are offering, their price, and the share of the company's equity you are planning to give up in return for this financing. If you are not seeking investors for your company, eliminate this section.

What Investors Look for in the Summary

Investors read the Summary first. Experienced investors and venture capitalists look for certain key indicators when reading a Summary. They look for something innovative, yet which also seems realistic based upon their experience. They also look for a management team that has successfully started and built a similar type of business. This doesn't mean it is impossible to succeed without this team of "old pros," just that it will be more difficult.

The experienced investor knows that some mistakes will be made without a core of experienced management. But he will also accept the fact that mistakes are a part of any business. What is most important to the investor is that management recognize that these mistakes will come about, and that they be ready to correct them quickly and efficiently. If a team has not been involved with a startup before, the Summary should refer to the fact that management understands the value of feedback and quick reaction to changes in the market. Doing so helps to relieve any fears the investor might have that you consider yourself infallible.

In discussing Unique Features, it is wise to allude to the competition. By doing so, you let the investor know that *you* are aware of what he already knows—that there *is* competition out there! Stress your product's or your service's single most unique quality and tell why it clearly stands out above the competition's. Most investors avoid "me too" products, so it's important that you distinguish yourself in the investor's eyes. Don't let the investor think you are naïve about the competition's capabilities.

All but the most gullible investors will have a good idea of what constitutes a reasonable dollar investment in your venture, and how much of the company stock should be exchanged for that investment. The three most common mistakes made by entrepreneurs in this area are

1. They fail to ask for enough funds—including "contingency" money and working capital—to adequately capitalize the company.

2. They are far too optimistic in their projections of sales and profits, and in the amount of cash their business will generate in its first several years. We have had clients who were very reluctantly convinced to *halve* their projected revenues for early years, and who were later astonished to find they *still* could not attain their projected levels.
3. The amount of equity in the company that the owner is willing to release to investors is too small to attract the necessary funds.

In Chapter Four, "Raising Money for Your Business," these topics are discussed in greater detail. Read the chapter carefully before deciding on the share of your company you want to offer to investors.

II. TABLE OF CONTENTS

The table of contents generally appears *after* the Summary, separating it from the body of the business plan. Use a standard format, an example of which can be found in this book.

III. BACKGROUND AND HISTORY OF THE COMPANY

III. Background and History of the Company
   A. How and Why the Company Was Formed
   B. How It Has Developed to Date
   C. Distinguishing Characteristics
   D. New Markets or Technologies Addressed
      by the Company
   E. Looking to the Future

This section tells a brief story about the company's history, and about the experiences of the members of your management team. Tell the story in a logical chronological sequence, leading right up to the present. Try to satisfy the reader's natural curiosity; be engaging but not long-winded.

A. How and Why the Company Was Formed

What caused you to become interested in this type of business in the first place? Was it a conversation, an article you read, an experience as a consumer, or a need you recognized from being in a related type of business? Describe the research you conducted to verify your initial ideas. If you had set-backs, honestly describe these as well.

B. How It Has Developed to Date

Bring the company up to its current status. If you have contacted suppliers or potential customers or staff, mention this and describe those contacts or arrangements. Include any other constructive activities in which the business has been involved.

C. Distinguishing Characteristics

What differentiates your company from all the rest? List the special talents or insights your team brings to the venture. Describe new marketing strategies that will bring attention to your company. Mention personal relationships or contacts within industry which will help open the right doors. This is the place to profile everything that makes your company unique.

As an example of unique strategies, consider two of the larger pizza chains, Little Caesar's and Domino's. The distinguishing characteristic of Domino's is its "fast and free" delivery service. It guarantees delivery within 30 minutes or it refunds the customer a certain amount. The distinguishing characteristic of Little Caesar's is its offer of "two for the price of one," which has begun a "two for one" battle in the industry. Each company's entire marketing effort is built around these distinct characteristics, which it hopes set it apart from its competitors.

D. New Markets or Technologies Addressed by the Company

If your company's products or services are aimed at a new or changing market, such as upwardly mobile professionals or the affluent elderly, this is the place to explain your strategy. You might be developing a technology which utilizes something new. Describe how that technology has developed, what it means to markets today and in the future. If you intend to approach some new market in the future, after your company has become established, describe this intention in the next section.

E. Looking to the Future

Everyone who is involved in the early stages of a startup company is anxious to see the business become a success. The attraction of a startup is that it promises a future of growth and profit. Your investors need to know that *your* company can give them that consistent growth and profit.

It's been said, "If you don't shoot for the stars, you won't make it to the moon." So let yourself go in this section of the business plan, and let the dreams run free. Create a scenario of what the future might hold. Any investor will know that the future, 10 years from now, can't be foretold with accuracy. But they want to see that you've got vision, and that you're not afraid to dream.

IV. PRODUCT(S) AND/OR SERVICE(S)

IV. Product(s) and/or Service(s)
   A. Present Products and/or Services
   B. Future Products and/or Services
   C. Why Will the Customer Buy?

This section is a detailed description of your company's product or service. Frequently, it is the longest section of the business plan, especially if the products are technical in nature. Drawings and photographs add an important element of realism and tangibility to the presentation. A plan can come to life when photos and artwork are used, personalizing an otherwise intangible product and creating a more memorable presentation.

If you have a prototype product, have it photographed by a professional industrial photographer. Photographs can be "screened" by the same print shop that makes the copies of your business plan when it is completed, so that they will be clearly reproduced in the final package.

If you are providing services instead of a product, photograph the facilities, equipment, or your employees. As an alternative, hire a commercial artist to illustrate settings depicting the service being rendered. These photos and illustrations are not mandatory, but they make your business plan more professional, and leave a lasting positive impression in the minds of potential investors.

A. Present Products and/or Services

List all the products and services your company is currently offering, or those which you plan to offer once operations have started. Be sure to give a complete description of the features of your products or services. Be clear and concise about their qualities, and their advantages over competitive products or services. This section will be carefully studied by prospective investors.

B. Future Products and/or Services

One of the best ways for a company to self-destruct is to rely upon only one product or service for its success. Even if a market is huge and competitors are nearly nonexistent (which is rarely the case), this situation won't exist for very long. When your company is successful it will lure others into the fray. Even an endless series of patents and copyrights cannot protect a company from this competition. The best defense is to diversify a company's products or service base.

Investors generally look for new products or services which are targeted toward the same customer base. These customers will always be the best targets for future products or services. So be sure to have several ideas for future products or services, and describe them in this section of the business plan.

C. Why Will the Customer Buy?

There are a number of standard answers to this question, such as "The price is right," "The quality is higher," or the old standbys "fast service" and "better workmanship." But *every-*

one gives these reasons. Why is the customer going to believe your claims over those of your competitors? Is it because of a marketing strategy you will employ, or because of a special means you're going to use to make the first sale to prospective customers? Back up any claims of faster service or higher quality with statistics from your research. Don't expect the reader to accept your claims without solid factual support.

V. THE MARKET

V. The Market
    A. Description of the Market
    B. Market Dynamics
    C. Secondary Markets
    D. Ongoing Market Testing

A. Description of the Market

Elaborate on the market niche you are pursuing, giving as much demographic and geographic description as possible. If you are offering complete automotive maintenance services from a fully equipped truck traveling to office complexes or homes, then your market will include families with two working spouses, busy executives, and perhaps elderly retired people who do not want to be without transportation for any period of time.

Look at the average income of each of these targeted groups in your geographic area. How much do they spend on auto repair? What is the average age of car they drive? (If they drove only new cars, perhaps the factory warranty would exclude you from servicing their vehicles.) Investors and lenders alike feel more secure when they can see you have put time and thought into fully analyzing your potential market.

B. Market Dynamics

Address any significant changes in the specific markets targeted for your product or service. These changes might be gradual trends, and could extend over the next 10 years. U.S. Department of Commerce reports are a good source for this information. Trade magazines and business journals are also useful sources for information on demographic changes. *Sales and Marketing Management* magazine is an excellent reference for this kind of information, as is *American Demographics* magazine.

Explain how you plan to modify your products, services, and marketing strategy to accommodate these changing markets. Investors and lenders will respect and value such far-sighted planning as an indication of a sophisticated approach to the future.

C. Secondary Markets

After you have established yourself in your initial market, there may be other markets open to your products and services. A startup mobile auto repair service company might plan on leaving the elderly out of the initial target market. They might be a potential future market, though. Identify the new markets you plan to approach, describe them, and then elaborate in this section on the strategy you will use to penetrate them.

D. Ongoing Market Testing

Large, successful companies such as Procter & Gamble are constantly doing market research and testing in order to discover what their market really wants. They learned long ago that it is impossible to guess consistently which product the public will want to buy. One mistake made by businesspeople is to believe the old adage, "Build a better mousetrap and the public will beat a path to your door." It just isn't so—it never has been and probably never will be.

The reasons a particular product attracts the interest of the public are often hard to decipher. Products which seem to be sure-fire winners in the hearts of consumers everywhere often fail quickly when launched in the marketplace.

A startup company must know what its customers want to buy. This section of the business plan describes the completed market testing, as well as future market testing and research. Groups of potential customers should be sampled—those who fit your buyer profile—to gauge their reaction to your product or service. They should be asked detailed questions about their preferences and feelings toward the product. A sample of one of these questionnaires, which can be created by yourself, should be included in the Appendix of your business plan. If you have trouble coming up with appropriate questions, do some quick research on market testing or opinion polls at the local library.

VI. COMPETITION

```
VI. Competition
    A. Description of Each Competitor
    B. Strengths & Weaknesses of the Competition
    C. Advantages over the Competition
    D. Anticipated Changes in the Competition
```

Just as there have always been death and taxes, so will there always be competition for those in the business world. Don't make light of that fact; take it very seriously. Once you accept the fact that your competitors are smart, well-financed, and probably already entrenched in the marketplace, you can go about the task of analyzing their potential weaknesses and strengths.

By knowing your enemies, you can develop the strategies you need to deal with them. By ignoring them, or convincing yourself that they don't exist, you condemn yourself to failure.

Ignoring the competition is an incredibly common mistake of first-time businesspeople, who are fond of saying, "There's no competition for my product." Such a businessperson is due for a rude surprise. Not only will competitors quickly appear (if they don't already exist) but they will steal the market away from you and quickly drive you out of business if ignored.

We were participating in the initial investigation (called a "due diligence" investigation) of a company that had been in business for a short time and was now seeking additional funding. When the owner was asked to name his major competitors, he responded, "We have no competition. In fact, we dominate our marketplace."

As part of this investigation, key potential customers of the business were asked where they made their purchases. Without exception, the two or three sources they gave did not include the company being researched. When asked to evaluate the product made by this company, they were unmerciful. They found it had no appreciable benefits in either pricing or performance. These potential customers indicated that they would not switch from their present suppliers.

Not only did this businessman not know his marketplace—his potential customers—but he also overestimated the attractiveness of his product to the consumer. As a result, he did not get the funding he sought; in fact he probably is no longer even in business. He made the fatal mistake of underestimating his competition.

Don't fall into this trap. By knowing your competitors, you will enjoy the confidence of your investors and lenders, who are sure to look closely for evidence that you have studied the competition. They will want you to tell them about the strengths and weaknesses of those competitors, and your advantages over them.

A. Description of Each Competitor

This section should be organized by the size of each of your competitors and by their geographic location. Their size can be determined in terms of their sales, number of locations, or their capitalization. Devote a brief section to each competitor, covering the differences in their products, prices, performance, quality, and service capabilities. Discuss their market shares, marketing strategies, and technological sophistication. Anything of significance you uncover about your competitor should be presented in this section.

B. Strengths and Weaknesses of the Competition

While the section above was arranged with a separate subsection for each competitor, this one should be arranged as a chart summarizing each competitor's individual strengths and weaknesses. Set up several columns for items such as "Financial Strength," "Number of Locations," and "Years in Business," and rate each competitor's relative strength on a scale of 1 to 10.

C. Advantages Over the Competition

After the analysis of your competition's strengths and weaknesses, you should be able to pinpoint the specific advantages your company will have over them. Compare your marketing and management approaches to theirs, with emphasis on how the differences will be perceived by the customer. Try to "hit 'em where they ain't" in the comparison between you and your competition, and establish your own niche in the marketplace.

D. Anticipated Changes in the Competition

Let the reader know in this section that you realize the importance of constantly monitoring your competition for changes in strategy that might affect you and your customers. How will your competition respond to your entry into their market? Will they lower their prices, or advertise more heavily? Obviously, this is mostly guesswork on your part, but you want the investor to know that you don't believe your competition is going to sit still forever, and that you will be ready for any changes in their strategy. You should read the trade news for reports of any mergers or closings that might affect your competition, and indicate in this section which magazines or journals you plan to monitor.

VII. SELLING TO THE MARKET

VII. Selling to the Market
    A. Sales Approach
    B. Advertising, Promotion, and Public Relations
    C. Delivering the Goods or Services
    D. Customer Feedback

You have identified your market, created a product or service that you feel will have great commercial appeal, and analyzed your competition. Now you have to decide how to tell potential customers about what you have to offer, and who is going to make the sale and follow up on the sale to be sure the customer is satisfied.

Too many inexperienced entrepreneurs give little or no thought to these important points, and they end up "winging it" after the business is started. This lack of thought shows in their sales, their profits, their image, and their level of customer satisfaction. The time to prepare your marketing strategy and sales tactics is *before* you open your doors, not after.

As an example, when the restaurant chain TGI Friday's was in its rapid expansion stage in the 70s and early 80s, it followed a specific format prior to each new grand opening. New personnel were carefully trained and rehearsed for days prior to the opening. The staff knew who the typical customers would be, how to handle them, and how to sell them special items that would increase the average amount each customer spent.

Because of this advance training, there were few missing orders, and no slow service. The efforts of the employees were calculated and rehearsed, and the first impressions were favorable from the customers' point of view. Seldom did a patron leave the restaurant dissatisfied with the service. Usually they became repeat customers and frequented TGI Friday's regularly. Management's intense preparation and planning paid off in a big way.

Don't discount the importance of the strategies you plan to use to service your customers, and don't discount the importance of this section of the business plan. The way products are sold and delivered to customers, the level of service provided, and the methods used to keep customers happy have *everything* to do with the ultimate success of a business.

A. Sales Approach

Describe the actual approach used by your company in selling to the customer. Are outside salespeople used, or do customers phone in or come to a showroom? Are the salespeople employed directly by your company, or are they independent agents? How are sales leads generated, and how are they handled? What selling points will be emphasized when dealing with prospects and customers? Will you approach them at their offices, or at their homes? This section should give the investor a general introduction to the type of marketing you will use.

B. Advertising, Promotion, and Public Relations

Describe the specific advertising ideas to be used, along with an explanation of the rationale behind them. Give details as to how much will be spent, and over what period of time. Remember that the financial projections will show the amounts to be spent on advertising and marketing, so be sure this section agrees with the financial information and explains it in some detail.

What are your long-term strategies, and what do you hope to accomplish by them? What types of public relations activities have you planned? Have you established methods of monitoring the results of various marketing approaches? A chart is often useful here, showing how much you expect to spend on radio, television, or printed advertising; direct mail; and special promotions.

C. Delivering the Goods or Services

If you own a retail store where people buy goods off your shelves, then delivery is easy: All you must do is hand over the merchandise. But in many businesses the sale is only the beginning. If you have to order something for the customer that's not already in stock, you must track the order and contact the customer when it arrives. Systems must be set up to do this. You also need a procedure for clearing customer payment. Will you accept personal checks? Will you accept credit cards? How will you protect your business from fraud?

If the products you sell are larger than a person would normally carry home, you must give thought to a method of delivery. Will you buy or lease a delivery truck? Is it more economical to contract with a local delivery service? What will its rates be? Who will insure the merchandise and how will claims be handled if the goods are damaged during delivery?

Another consideration is service. Will you hire your own installation and service personnel, or will you, as Sears does for much of its service, use subcontractors? If you're going to do the latter, you will need agreements covering liability and quality. You can always amend your system later, but the reader of the business plan needs to know that you've examined these areas.

D. Customer Feedback

By paying close attention to the feedback you get from your customers, you will earn yourself distinction in their minds and build loyal repeat business. Just think about this for a moment: You've been a customer many times; have you ever had anyone call you to see if you liked the product you bought? If this has ever happened, you'd most likely remember it. It makes you feel important as a customer; someone really cares about your satisfaction.

This means more than just form letters. They may be better than nothing, but they're too impersonal to make a lasting impression, and making a lasting and positive impression is just what you want to do. Obtaining customer feedback will be one of the most effective things you will do to bring in more business— more effective than the lowest prices in the city. But it has to be done correctly. Give some careful thought to how you're going to seek customer feedback, and to how you're going to respond to it. Be sure to *ask your customers* what they like, as well as what they *don't* like about the product or service you've sold them, and be prepared to take corrective steps if the response is negative.

In 1982 one of your authors bought a new car. About two weeks after taking delivery he received a phone call from the dealership which made the sale, and an elderly woman introduced herself as a "customer relations" representative. She proceeded to thank the author for buying the car from them, and asked if there were any problems with it.

In fact, there had been recurring problems with the brakes and the paint, and the author was relieved to find that someone was finally interested in these problems, especially since the car had been taken to the dealership several times with no success. The woman listened patiently while the problems were explained to her, but then told the author apologetically that her only job was to call the customers. To have any work done, he would have to visit the service department—which he had already done on several occasions. This brought the author back to square one. The call was not transferred, as you might expect, to the service manager, the owner, or the service department, and there was no offer to help solve these problems.

This half-hearted attempt at customer relations certainly cost the car dealership any future business from the frustrated writer. Worse, this particular story was told time and again whenever the subject of buying cars came up among friends and associates.

As you read this section, stop and think how many times *you* have been a frustrated and disappointed customer. You can probably identify with the story of the car dealer above. It would have been easy for the dealer to have instructed the person calling customers to transfer any problems or complaints to a particular employee, whose responsibility it would be to follow up on those problems and ensure customer satisfaction.

Management's response to customer feedback is the key to building a good business reputation, and it warrants serious thought. How will you get customer feedback in your business? Obviously, not all types of businesses lend themselves to the possibility of personal phone calls or direct contact, but if yours does, you should set up a system to take advantage of it. Stay in touch with your customers! *Word of mouth* always leads the polls as the most effective form of advertising, so be sure it works *for* you and not *against* you.

VIII. MANUFACTURING THE PRODUCT (OR CREATING THE SERVICE)

> VIII. Manufacturing the Product (or Creating the Service)
> A. Suppliers
> B. Physical Facilities
> C. Personnel
> D. Warehousing
> E. Quality Control and Warranty

A. Suppliers

Every company has its suppliers, whether for office supplies, raw materials for manufacturing, finished goods for resale, or subcontracted services. In this section of the business plan you should describe which suppliers you have chosen to work with, and what makes them the best choice. Invest a little time in researching the various suppliers in your area. Obtain price quotes or lists, and visit the suppliers if possible. Get a general impression of the people you'll be working with, and inquire about their credit policies and their warranty and service procedures. Keep your impressions in a notebook. This will be very helpful to you later, when you make your final choices.

B. Physical Facilities

Most likely you are going to need an office or work area from which to run your business. You might be planning to start out in your home; but if you expect your business to grow, your plans will have to include an office, or a place to make your products. If you have the time, try to find a definite location for your facilities or offices, and get a letter of commitment from the landlord of the property. Include this letter in the Appendix of your business plan and refer to it here. This also gives you a firm dollar amount to use as lease expense on your projected financial statements.

Describe the physical advantages of the location you have chosen. Even if you haven't found a specific location and entered into a lease or obtained a letter of commitment, you still should have a general idea of the current lease rates and conditions in the geographic area you have chosen. Describe some of the related plant or office costs such as utilities, insurance, repairs, real estate taxes, and leasehold improvements. Include a floor plan of the space you will need, with all the desks, file cabinets, work tables, and so on, that you must have to run the company. By anticipating all these details, you go far in avoiding some of the delays which plague many entrepreneurial startups.

C. Personnel

It takes people to make products or provide services, and they all don't just suddenly appear at your doorstep on the day you open for business. You must anticipate the number of employees you'll need, and their specific skills. You must be familiar with the wage and pay scale in your area and industry, so that you can reasonably estimate your total expenses for staff. Make a complete list of all the positions you expect to have in your firm, and assign a wage and benefit package to each position. Summarize such information in this section of the business plan, and also use the amounts you have calculated in your financial projections.

D. Warehousing

If you only provide a service, you will want to skip this section entirely, unless your service requires the storage of equipment when not in use. But if you're in manufacturing, you need a place to store your product until it is shipped. Don't overlook this important need.

E. Quality Control and Warranty

Whatever you do, make, or sell, you should establish customer satisfaction as the first priority. Without customer satisfaction you will generate negative goodwill, which will outweigh any amount of advertising you might do. The most important thing you can do in business is to keep your customers satisfied: It will keep you standing head and shoulders above the competition. The first step toward achieving this level of satisfaction is treating the customer as if you appreciate his or her business. The second is selling a product or service that is fairly priced. The third is making sure that the product meets stringent quality standards, and the fourth—and most important by far—is satisfying the customer when a problem arises.

If something doesn't work properly, fix it promptly with no argument or question. This may sound simple, but it isn't, because the human ego is involved. Customer complaints become a "game" in which you, as the businessperson, believe every customer is trying to get something for nothing and take advantage of you. But this is rarely so. Sure, customers may exaggerate their complaints, but they've learned they *have* to do this with most businesses in order to get a satisfactory response. Ignore their little deceptions and take care of their problems with a smile (and have everyone in your company do the same).

The number of people experiencing problems will always be small, but they can be a vociferous minority. And even if the problem is really only in their own minds, they nonetheless feel let down. Help them solve their problems, and you gain loyal customers who will recommend you to others. They become unpaid salespeople.

So establish a stringent quality control procedure. Customers today want *quality*, and if something does happen to go wrong with your product or service, stand behind it with a strong, fair warranty. Above all, satisfy your customers.

IX. COMPANY STRUCTURE

IX. Company Structure
   A. The Business Entity
   B. Ownership of the Company
   C. Anticipated Changes in the Business Structure
   D. Public Offering Possibilities

A. The Business Entity

When starting a new business, you can choose one of several business forms: a proprietorship, a partnership or a limited partnership, a corporation or an S corporation. The form you choose will profoundly influence the desirability of the business from an outside investor's point of view, as well as the overall flexibility of your company. This decision is one that must be given a great deal of careful thought.

Read Chapter Three to find out about the advantages and disadvantages of each form, and then discuss the decision with your attorney and accountant. After you've decided which form to use, explain that decision in this section of your business plan, emphasizing the points which are most important to your investors.

B. Ownership of the Company

This section of the business plan deals with who owns what, both as the company exists today (unless it's a startup company) and as it will appear after the current offering to investors. Ownership should be shown by both the number of shares or partnership interests owned, and by the percentage of the whole company that the ownership represents.

If you have a corporation, remember that only the *issued* shares represent an ownership percentage: For example, you might have *authorized* 100,000 shares of stock (meaning there are 100,000 available for distribution, including what's already distributed), but only *issued* 1,000 of those shares. If this is the case, someone owning 500 shares will have a 50 percent ownership of the company. Table 2–1 shows a standard format for presentation of this information. The names of the current stockholders don't necessarily have to be listed in this section (although they often are). Until you have generated some inter-

TABLE 2–1
Format for Reporting on Ownership

	Current Stock Ownership	
	Number of Shares Held	*Percentage Owned*
Stockholder A	3,000	30%
Stockholder B	1,500	15
Stockholder C	3,500	35
Stockholder D	2,000	20
Total	10,000	100%

	Projected Ownership After Current Offering	
	Number of Shares Held	*Percentage Owned*
Stockholder A	3,000	15.0%
Stockholder B	1,500	7.5
Stockholder C	3,500	17.5
Stockholder D	2,000	10.0
New Investors	10,000	50.0
Total	20,000	100.0%

est from a prospective lender or investor, it might be best to keep those names undisclosed, unless you feel the names would be particularly influential ones. Don't hesitate to name them, though, should you get a legitimate request to do so.

C. Anticipated Changes in the Business Structure

This is an optional section, to be used if you plan to change your business form in the future. If you started out as a partnership but plan to reorganize as a corporation, or if you are planning on being an S corporation for only the first year or two and then changing to a normal corporation, you would explain that strategy here. Your corporate structure might also need to be changed if you plan to acquire other businesses. If you are able to anticipate, with some certainty, changes in your legal form, these should be addressed in this section.

D. Public Offering Possibilities

Starting or buying a business, and then building that business into a flourishing, money-making company, is challenging and exciting. You reap financial rewards and enjoy the many benefits of success. But what about your investors? When does their payday come?

For many, the big payday arrives when a company goes public and sells shares to the general public. Stock that had been purchased for a few pennies a share might be sold for several dollars. The public offering can be the pot of gold at the end of the rainbow for your investors. Many success stories have been written about the initial investors who cashed in their stock for millions in profits. This is the big lure for higher-risk investors.

A public offering can also be rewarding for the entrepreneur who took the company from its startup or acquisition to maturity. So always plan your growth and expansion with an eye toward the possibility of taking your company public. Keep notes and clippings from magazines such as *Forbes, Inc., Business Week, Fortune,* and *Venture* and from newspapers such as *The Wall Street Journal,* which tell of companies similar to yours that have issued shares to the public. These stories illustrate that successful public offerings *are* possible. They also give an indication of what these companies are worth.

A future public offering is a powerful inducement to a prospective investor. Mentioning it as a possibility is an absolute must in a business plan that is used to raise money from outside investors.

X. THE PEOPLE

> X. The People
>   A. Resumes of Founders and Key Employees
>   B. Organizational Chart
>   C. Job Descriptions of Key Employees
>   D. Directors and Major Stockholders

From our experience as advisers to venture capitalists and investment bankers, we've learned that there are several sections of a business plan that are read immediately. One of these is the section describing the people behind the company. This section is extremely important, especially to professional investors.

Ideally, the people holding the key positions in a company, especially a startup, should complement each other. A baseball team consisting only of pitchers might have a strong pitching game, but they'll be consistently clobbered by the competition because they won't have the hitting and fielding that make for a well-rounded team. A company is no different. A management team consisting of all salespeople will sell a lot of product, at least at first, but will probably devote little effort to things like product quality, manufacturing efficiency, storage and shipment, or collections and bookkeeping. Such a company will not last long.

The ideal management team has several attributes.

1. *Experience* in the same or a very similar business as that the new company is going into and, better yet, past experience in a startup that was successful.
2. *Maturity*, from having been through at least one com-

plete economic cycle of expansion and recession, which teaches that things never stay the same—that a company must deal with tough times as well as good ones.
3. A *history* of success in other endeavors, showing that the individuals know what it takes to succeed.
4. *Diversified* and complementary backgrounds covering administration, sales and marketing, production, and finance.

If all these qualities are present in the team you have selected, you're on the right track. If, on the other hand, your team falls short on one or more of these attributes, perhaps you should take a few steps back and reassess the team. Finding the right people increases your chances for success many times over. The professional investors know this, and that's why they look for it in a new company. You too should look for it in your own business.

A. Resumes of Founders and Key Employees

Once you have found the right people, use this section of the business plan to illustrate *why* they are the right people. Informative resumes will tell this story. This type of resume is not done in a standard format, however. Most standard resumes are written as part of a basic employment application, and that won't do for this section. Your business plan resumes are going to be written mostly in prose, briefly describing the relevant experiences, education, and accomplishments of the key managers. In other words, they not only give dates, positions, and names of employers, they also tell a story. Who you worked for and when is really not as important as *what you did while you were there*. Don't get into too much detail. Just be sure that the relevant, important, and *impressive* points are made. More detailed and traditional resumes should be included in the Appendix.

B. Organizational Chart

Some office supply stores sell blank organizational charts, or you can create one with a felt-tipped pen. This chart illustrates the chain of command and the various responsibilities of each individual on your team. Organizational charts are

FIGURE 2–1
A Typical Organizational Chart

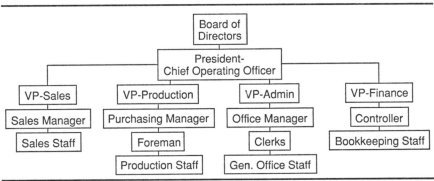

excellent visual representations of otherwise ambiguous divisions of responsibility within a company. It will help your key people understand their areas of responsibility and it will show investors that your thoughts and plans are well-organized. A typical organizational chart might look like Figure 2–1.

C. Job Descriptions of Key Employees

Job descriptions need not be an elaborate undertaking, but they are important because they force you to think about the specific roles and responsibilities your staff is going to take on. These general descriptions will also help you with your hiring efforts, making you fill specific slots rather than searching for poorly defined qualifications in job applicants. The descriptions should include a brief outline of the responsibilities of each key employee, the skills necessary to fill the job, and the salary levels and bonus incentive programs you have planned. There are many salary surveys published in business magazines, and you can enlist the help of your accountant to determine salary levels in your area.

D. Directors and Major Stockholders

Assuming you have a corporation, the Board of Directors you choose is going to be an important factor in gaining recognition within the business community and among potential investors. In

Chapter Ten, "Managing a Business for Maximum Profit," we discuss the best people to get for your Board. This is the place in the business plan to describe those whom you have chosen, and to highlight their experience and accomplishments. Similarly, you might want to give a little background on your major stockholders: The fact that a respected investor would think enough of your plans and abilities to put money into your venture is an excellent endorsement, and this is the place to take credit for it.

XI. FINANCIALS

XI. Financials
    A. Use of Proceeds Statement
    B. Five-Year Projections (Forecasted Financial
       Statements)
    C. Recent Financial Statements

The section of your business plan which deals with financial projections is one of the most important, and will probably be the first section investors look at after the Summary and Resumes of Founders and Key Employees. We have devoted Chapter Five to financial statements. This chapter explains the statements that are to be included in the business plan. It also emphasizes an important point—your financial statements should be prepared only with the help of a qualified professional. This ensures that the potential investor doesn't have to scrutinize some customized format of your own creation, but can look at the various statements and immediately understand them. A brief summary of what these statements contain follows, but a better explanation is found in Chapter Five.

A. "Use of Proceeds" Statement

This is generally the first of the financial statements, and is immediately followed by "Notes," which give greater detail. The statement allows investors to tell, at a glance, exactly where the requested money is to be spent.

B. Five-year Projections (Forecasted Financial Statements)

These projections are your estimates of revenues, costs, and earnings for the company over the next five years, and they are followed by several pages of "Assumptions" used in the projections. These projections allow the investor to gauge your potential profitability and cash flow, and are used by the investor to determine what the company might be worth in the future.

C. Recent Financial Statements

These statements would only be included if your company is *not* a startup, but has been in operation for some time. It's best if these statements have been prepared less than six months prior to the date the business plan is completed. That way, all the financial information is reasonably current.

XII. APPENDIX

XII. Appendix
    A. Legal and Accounting Relationships
    B. Banking Relationships
    C. Detailed Resumes of Key People
    D. Sources for Facts or Figures
    E. Letters of Recommendation and References
    F. Suppliers' Price Lists, Quotes,
    G. Market Testing Information
    H. Technical Information
     I. Other Matters and Items

The Appendix is for information or attachments that support or expand on topics already covered in the body of the business plan. Everything in this section is, to a certain extent, optional, but it's best to give as much critical information as you can. The investor can easily find whatever information he or she wants, while ignoring that which *isn't* needed. The contents of the Appendix help to make it clear that you have ample support for the representations you've made in the business plan.

A. Legal and Accounting Relationships

If your attorneys and accountants are partners in a prominent firm, they will most likely have brochures describing their firms, and you will want to attach these brochures, or photocopies of them, in this portion of the Appendix. You might also want to describe the individual attorney or accountant assigned by their firm as the "partner-in-charge" of your business. An engagement letter from the law firm or accounting firm—stating that they have agreed to provide you with certain professional services— might also be appropriate in this section.

B. Banking Relationships

Every business must have a bank to deal with, and many established businesses deal with several banks. Each bank can be an important reference for you, so you should begin to set up personal relationships with the officers of these banks. The branch manager is your first contact, and you should make it a point to introduce yourself, explaining your business and summarizing your plans. Stay visible to the manager, so he or she will not forget who you are. You should also ask to be introduced to a commercial lending officer, even if you are not anticipating a bank loan at the time. Ask the lending officer to describe the types of loans available, and their costs, interest rates, and procedures. After you've met these bank officers, ask their permission to include their names and titles in this section of your business plan. If you've had prior dealings with these officers, ask for a letter of recommendation to include here. Good banking relations add to your credibility considerably; no banking relations at all indicate a lack of business experience or, worse, bad past experiences with banks.

C. Detailed Resumes of Key People

Earlier in this business plan, in Section X, you included summary resumes of your key people and founders. In this section you should back up those brief, narrative resumes with specific details about the experiences and accomplishments each has had. These resumes, like those in Section X, should not read like an employment application, but should have much more detail than the earlier section. Remember the reason for the resumes is to sell the reader (the investor or lender) on the ability of these people (yourself included) to work together to achieve the goals of the business and the bottom line profitability projected in the financial statements.

D. Sources for Facts and Figures

If you state in the manufacturing section of the business plan that you can make a product for a specific cost, you should include supporting data in this section of the Appendix. If, for instance, you base your assumptions on population growth projections found in a Department of Commerce study, you should include a photocopy of the page of the study where the projections were shown and highlight them, so that they're easy to see. Charts and graphs are always interesting and credible forms of illustration, and are a great addition to business plans. While doing your research, you're bound to come across many charts. Photocopy them or clip them out for inclusion here in the Appendix. Your objective in compiling all these facts, figures, maps, charts, and graphs is to give credibility to your plans and projections. *Don't lose your credibility by making exaggerated or unsubstantiated claims, because if you're caught doing this, then everything else you say will be suspect too.* Establish your credibility early, and you've won an important battle and gained a distinct advantage. A well-done, thorough section that provides the source of your facts and figures is indispensable.

E. Letters of Recommendation and References

Like the previous sections, the purpose of this section is to establish your credibility and that of your co-founders and key employees. Each person involved in the venture should ask for letters from businesspeople who have worked with him or her in the past. You will want an endorsement of their honesty, intelligence, and energy, their accomplishments, and their ability to do what they say they can do. If you can't get a letter from someone, ask if his or her name can be included as a reference. These letters might also include comments from customers endorsing your product or service. If your business is in the startup stage, you may want to seek letters from *prospective* customers stating their desire to buy your products and use your services once they become available.

F. Suppliers' Price Lists, Quotes

Include copies of price lists or quotes from suppliers or prospective suppliers. It's wise to have a few prices on the same items or services—it shows that you have shopped around a bit in trying to obtain the best price. Documentation of suppliers' interest in working with you, including correspondence from them and credit terms you've been offered, is also a good addition.

G. Market Testing Information

We encourage you to do some market testing before you decide to launch a product or service. Market testing is essentially asking potential customers whether or not they would be interested in buying your product or using your service, and, if so, what price they would be willing to pay. Keep careful records of the questions asked, who was asked, what the responses were, and the conclusions reached as a result of this market testing.

If you are unable to conduct this market testing yourself, you may be able to find similar tests that were already conducted by searching the reference material and periodicals at your library. Or, you could go to the expense of hiring a professional market research firm, although this is an expensive proposition. As an alternative, you could check with the business school of a large university in the area. Often they will have upper division advertising and marketing classes that will conduct market research at very reasonable costs. The intelligent businessperson will make certain that the market actually wants the product or service he intends to offer, and is willing to pay for it. This section of the Appendix offers evidence of that market testing.

H. Technical Information

If your product is technical in nature, this is where the greatest part of the technical information should be presented. Too much technical information or terminology in the body of the plan tends to bore the reader, so confine the bulk of it to this area.

I. Other Matters and Items

It's impossible for us to anticipate all the information, documentation, and exhibits that you will need for your particular product or service. You will probably have other material unique to your business to include in the Appendix. This is as it should be, for every product or service is special in some respect. Whatever your needs, simply continue as we've done above, using whatever titles best fit your material. Remember, the readers are going to refer only to those sections of the Appendix they *need* to refer to, so don't worry about overdoing it.

By the time you have assembled all the information that goes into the business plan, you will be an authority on your proposed business and on the industry in which it will operate. This range of knowledge will help you impress potential investors and lenders, helping you to become a success in your chosen field. While your competitors may be caught off guard by new developments in your industry or by new marketing techniques, *you* will be prepared to take advantage of these changes or developments.

The time and effort invested in your business plan will have given you a distinct and sizable advantage over the competition. And such advantages will lead to success in business startups.

CHAPTER 3

CHOOSING THE
RIGHT FORM OF BUSINESS

Proprietorships, Partnerships, and Corporations

In This Chapter:

1. Forms of business
2. Sole proprietorship: The one-man show
3. Partnerships: General and Limited
4. Corporations

FORMS OF BUSINESS

There are several types of legal structures available for you to use when starting a business; each has distinct advantages and disadvantages depending upon your unique circumstances. The most common of these structures are the sole proprietorship, the partnership, and the corporation. It's important that you put careful thought into the form that will work best for you. Both your attorney, for legal reasons, and your accountant, for tax reasons, should be involved in the decision-making process. This chapter gives you a brief introduction to the most common business structures, and outlines their general advantages and disadvantages.

SOLE PROPRIETORSHIP: THE ONE-MAN SHOW

A sole proprietorship requires no formal agreement of any kind, for there are no partners or other parties involved; only one person does business for his or her own benefit. As such, a sole proprietorship is certainly the simplest form of business to operate and the least costly to begin. Of course, you have to be able to supply your own startup capital, or be willing and able to personally borrow it, for there isn't any way to give up part of the ownership of a sole proprietorship to an interested investor; as soon as you do that, your proprietorship would become a partnership. But for many very small businesses, especially those started in homes and garages, the sole proprietorship is the preferred form of business, if only by default.

Besides the minimal cost of beginning a sole proprietorship, another major reason for its popularity is the simplicity of reporting it for income tax purposes. There is no complicated separate tax return for sole proprietorships, and no separate tax on the business's earnings, as there is with a corporation. All the revenues and expenses of the business are reported on a simple tax form (Schedule "C") which is attached to your personal income tax return. If the business generates a profit, that profit is added to your personal taxable income (from wages, interest earned, etc.). If there is a loss, the loss is subtracted from your income, and your personal tax liability is computed in the usual way.

The major problem with sole proprietorships is one of liability. As a sole proprietor, you have absolutely no protection from legal actions brought by customers, suppliers, or the general public. If you are sued by a customer for any reason—from product liability to personal injury—nothing stands between you and potential financial ruin, except the amount and quality of whatever insurance you may own. And it's costly and difficult—probably impossible—to have insurance against every possible contingency.

Let's say you decide to open a small business and you elect to operate as a sole proprietor (actually, by electing *not* to become a corporation, and not bringing in any partners, you've automatically *become* a sole proprietorship). You rent a small office space and purchase the equipment you need, and begin advertising your services.

Over a period of several years, your business grows and your profits build and you are pleased with your progress. Then, one day, a potential customer (or maybe the paperboy) trips and falls upon entering your office. He claims permanent disability and sues you for $500,000.

Unless you're fully insured against this, you are going to have full potential *personal* liability for the claim. Even if the lawsuit is a meritless one, the cost of defending yourself could be staggering. The law makes no distinction between your business assets and your personal assets if you are a sole proprietorship, and, should you lose the lawsuit, the $500,000 settlement can not only attach the assets of the business, but also your *private holdings*: your personal stock portfolio, savings accounts, personal belongings, maybe even your car or your house.

The amount potentially at risk in a sole proprietorship can be massive, and much more than most sole proprietors realize. Risk, therefore, is the principal argument against the sole proprietorship as a form of business.

PARTNERSHIPS: GENERAL AND LIMITED

The General Partnership

A partnership is created as soon as any two or more parties reach an agreement on the operation of a business. A partnership can legally be formed without a written agreement, but all serious business partnerships are formed around what is known as a "Partnership Agreement." This document sets the rules on how the partnership will operate.

The major advantage of partnerships (as in sole proprietorships) is that the taxable income and losses of the business are passed through to the partners individually. The partnership itself pays no tax on profits, so there is no double taxation, as may be found in corporations. Whatever taxable income is generated by the partnership is simply added to the taxable income of the partners, based upon their partnership interest or as determined by the partnership agreement. This income is taxed much as if it were wages earned through a regular job. Likewise, losses of the partnership are passed through to the partners directly, and these losses reduce the amount of income on which the partners must pay tax.

Another related advantage of partnerships is that the distribution of the partnership's profits and losses to the partners does *not* have to be in the same ratio as their ownership of the assets of the business. For example, a person might want to put together a business which would be operated single-handedly, but for which investment capital was needed. This entrepreneur could approach a friend or relative for the money to get started, and establish the business as a partnership. Even though the investor put in 100 percent of the money, the ownership of partnership assets might be established at 50 percent–50 percent. However, because the investor most likely has a higher taxable income than the fledgling businessperson, the partnership agreement might stipulate that any tax *losses* would belong to the investor, while taxable *income* would be split 50–50. This type of arrangement can sometimes be helpful in convincing an investor to participate in a business deal— especially if the business is likely to have a year or two of losses before becoming profitable.

But the same thing which allows the profits and losses to be distributed in whatever manner you elect (subject to some general IRS rules) is at the heart of a major problem with partnerships: Because partnerships have no legal existence *except* through the agreement of the partners, *everything* which has a bearing on the partnership should be addressed in the legal agreement. Nothing can be taken for granted, and every contingency must be covered. This includes such details as which partner will be responsible for daily operations; what those operations will be; what records will be kept and who will keep them; how often financial reports will be done; how tax losses and income will be distributed; and what happens if one or more of the partners withdraws or dies. The list of options is almost endless, and many partnership agreements wind up being page after page of grueling detail. An experienced business attorney is best able to construct one of these cumbersome documents. Also, be aware that the cost of its preparation can exceed—by a wide margin—the cost of incorporation.

A second major problem with partnerships also springs from their reliance upon a partnership agreement: Once one of the partners dies or withdraws, the partnership ceases to exist. The partnership has no legal existence of its own, independent of the partners. It is only their *agreement* that keeps it alive.

The third problem with partnerships is a lack of protection from business liabilities. For regular partnerships, this problem is magnified, for *each* partner is held responsible for 100 percent of the liabilities of the partnership, *regardless* of the percentage of the business each owns.

For example, assume you decide to go into business with a friend in a retail video tape store. Each of you takes 50 percent of the partnership, but *you* put in the $50,000 cash to get things started, while your friend agrees to work at a minimal wage until things become profitable. Your partnership agreement states that you will both be equally liable for any debts of the business.

Shortly after getting underway, your partner decides to take advantage of a supplier's offer of financing, and orders an additional $50,000 in tapes on credit, agreeing to pay for them in 90 days. But things do not go well for the store, and sales are far less than expected. On top of it all, your friend becomes disheartened and suffers an emotional breakdown, totally mismanaging the store. By the time the 90 days have expired, the store has no extra cash, and its remaining inventory is nearly worthless. Your friend is resting at home.

Unfortunately for you, the company which sold your store the tapes on credit is going to look to *you* for the $50,000 it is owed. It makes no difference to them that your ownership of the partnership is only 50 percent (it wouldn't have mattered if it had been only 10 percent), or that you have an agreement with your partner that each of you will only bear half of any losses. They can go after either of you to collect their money, and they're going to most actively pursue the one with the most money. Of course, you'll be able to sue your friend for his half of the losses—but that may not be much of a consolation.

In addition to the normal debts of the partnership, you may also be held liable for acts of negligence committed by your partners. Especially in today's litigious society—where law suits are as common as fast foods—unlimited liability is a serious consideration for a businessperson.

The Limited Partnership

The Limited Partnership was created principally to avoid the problem of unlimited legal liability inherent in the general partnership, while retaining some of the tax features of that form. It accomplishes this by establishing two different classes of partners. The first is the "General Partner(s)," whose job it is to run the day-to-day operations of the partnership. The General Partner, which can be an individual or a corporation, carries the same broad legal liability as does any partner in a regular partnership—unlimited personal liability for the legal debts of the partnership. The second class is "Limited Partners," who, as the name implies, have only limited liability for the debts of, and claims against, the partnership—usually limited to the amount of money they have invested in it. Limited Partners are legally prevented from taking any type of active role in the management of the partnership—that role is reserved solely for General Partners.

It may occur to you to ask, "Why not make *all* the partners Limited Partners?" The answer is simply that the law *requires* each limited partnership to have at least one General Partner. The Limited Partnership is at least as complicated to establish as is the regular partnership, and, like corporations, it must be registered with the state, thereby making the cost of a Limited Partnership fairly high. The form has in the past been used most often for tax shelters, because it allowed the tax losses and tax credits of a business to flow through to the partners directly (just as they would in a general partnership) while giving the limited partners much of the legal protection of a corporation.

CORPORATIONS

The Regular Corporation

This is the most common form of business for companies larger than a one-person operation. A corporation is a very special type of business organization created by state law; the corporation is given a life all its own. The corporation becomes an artificial person in the eyes of the law, and as long as the required annual fees are paid and the corporation follows the rules and regulations set by the state of incorporation, it will live indefinitely, even after the death of its original owners. This is one of the major advantages of the corporation over the general partnership or the sole proprietorship: Because the corporation does not depend upon an agreement between the owners, as does a partnership, it continues to exist whether or not the original owners remain active. This allows ownership in the corporation to be easily bought, sold, or otherwise transferred.

A corporation can have one or many owners—there are no restrictions on how many people may own an interest in it. To start a corporation, a person has merely to select a name that isn't already registered, file a notice of incorporation with the proper state agency, pay certain fees, and complete some paperwork. Most states require that you appoint and maintain what is called a "registered agent," which gives the state a means of contacting the corporation.

The corporation will authorize a certain number of shares of stock, each share usually representing a particular percentage ownership of the whole corporation. The corporation's daily affairs are managed by its officers, who are appointed by a Board of Directors, who, in turn, have been elected by a majority of the stockholders.

This may sound as if you're required to have dozens of people in the corporation, just to fill all these roles, but that really isn't the case at all. In many states, one person can start a corporation, issue all the stock to herself, elect herself to the Board of Directors (or elect not to have a Board), and appoint herself president, secretary, and treasurer. All states are not the same in their requirements, however, and some require at least two officers, although they may be husband and wife. Be sure to check with an attorney before finalizing your plans.

The major advantage of the corporation over either the partnership or the sole proprietorship is the protection it provides its owners against the legal and financial liabilities of the business. Unless the stockholders have personally guaranteed certain liabilities, their risk is limited to the amount of their investment in the corporation.

If the corporation gets into financial trouble, its creditors can attach only the assets of the corporation. The individual stockholders are off limits. This same rule holds true for lawsuits for personal injury or product liability: No matter how large the lawsuit, the personal assets of the stockholders are safe from seizure as long as the stockholders weren't guilty of fraud or gross negligence.

This one feature—limited personal liability for the owners—should be important enough, by itself, to recommend the corporation as the form of business to be preferred where possible. But all is not perfect with this form either, for corporations have their own inherent and often costly problem—double taxation.

The normal corporation, unlike the sole proprietorship (or any form of partnership) is taxed on the income it earns. This is the price it pays for being treated as an entity legally separate from its owners. The tax rate applicable to corporations changes every few years, but its average rate usually hovers around 30 percent. So the price it pays through taxation isn't cheap.

The real problem comes, though, when the corporation distributes its after-tax profits to its owners. These distributions of profits are called "dividends," and dividends become taxable income to the stockholders, who receive them just as if they were interest earned on a savings account. This means the stockholders have been taxed twice: Once at the corporation's rate and then again at the stockholders' personal tax rates. This is called "double taxation."

There are two ways that double taxation can be avoided. The first method works only for corporations with a small group of stockholders. Each of these stockholders must be active in the management of the company, and the corporation's annual net income must be less than a certain amount. (Since tax laws change frequently, an accountant should be asked to verify current rulings on maximum net income level.) In these cases, the net profits of the company can be paid out to the stockholder/ managers as salaries. Salaries are a tax-deductible expense for the corporation (whereas dividends are not), so the corporation ends up with no taxable income.

The limitation on this solution is that the salaries, according to the IRS, must be "reasonable" to be deductible. If the IRS determines that a particular officer's salary is too high (compared to what comparable employees receive in similar companies), then they treat the excess salary as dividends, thereby thwarting the stockholder's intention. Naturally, salaries vary widely from case to case, with amounts as high as several hundred thousand dollars not necessarily being considered "unreasonable," but it's best to discuss these limitations with your accountant before trying to second-guess the IRS.

And this solution won't work at all for corporations with silent investors who aren't part of active management. These passive investors can't claim a salary (they haven't performed any work), and they would certainly have qualms about the active officers taking out all the profits as salaries for themselves.

The second method that can be used to avoid double taxation is to make an election with the IRS—on a one-time basis—which allows the corporation to *avoid* being taxed as a normal one. This option isn't open to all corporations, but for those to whom it is, it can be a genuine boon. The election is established by the Internal Revenue Code under a section known as Subchapter S, and corporations which elect to be taxed under the provisions of this section are known as S corporations.

The S Corporation

In every respect *except tax treatment*, S corporations are identical to normal corporations. This means that all the advantages unique to corporations are preserved, while the potential tax problems are eliminated. But when the stockholders of a corporation elect to be taxed under these special provisions, their corporation is no longer taxed separately as an individual entity (as are other corporations). Instead, the net income or loss of the corporation is passed through to the stockholders just as if the business were a partnership. The corporation pays no tax itself, and the stockholders add their pro rata share of the income or loss to their own taxable income, paying tax at their personal rates. Thus, double taxation is eliminated.

Not every corporation may be taxed as an S corporation. To qualify, a corporation must have less than a certain number of stockholders (35 at the date of writing). None of the stockholders can be a corporation, partnership, or a nonresident alien. The S corporation is not allowed to own more than 80 percent of another corporation, and it can't have more than one class of stock (such as preferred stock and common stock together).

Most small corporations, though, especially those in the startup stage, won't find that these restrictions apply to them. It's no coincidence, for example, that the limitation of 35 stockholders is the same number usually allowed before a stock offering must be registered with the Securities and Exchange Commission (SEC). And if a corporation grows to the point that it *does* violate one of these restrictions, then its status as an S corporation is simply terminated, and it becomes a regular corporation. In fact, as a corporation grows, it becomes less and less likely that it will *want* to remain an S corporation.

The S corporation status is especially advantageous during the first year or two of operations, when a company often incurs startup losses. In a regular corporation the stockholders receive no direct benefit from these losses, because the loss is not passed through to them. Instead, losses build up on the corporation's books until they eventually offset corporate income in the future (assuming there *are* profits in the future). The S corporation stockholders, however, can write off their share of losses in the years these occur, thus gaining significant personal tax savings.

As the number of stockholders involved in the corporation grows, the requirement for reporting each of the stockholder's pro rata share of taxable income becomes a burden for the corporation. Many of these new stockholders may not like the idea of having an uncertain amount of corporate income added to their personal income each year. Usually the S corporation

TABLE 3–1
Attributes of Major Business Forms

	Sole Proprietorship	General Partnership	Limited Partnership	Normal Corporation	S Corporation
Easy to start	Yes	No	No	Yes	Yes
Easy to operate	Yes	No	Yes	Yes	Yes
Inexpensive to start	Yes	No	No	Yes	Yes
Continues after owners' death	No	No	Yes	Yes	Yes
Easy to sell ownership interest	No	No	No	Yes	Yes
Limited legal and financial liability	No	No	Yes	Yes	Yes
Taxed only once	Yes	Yes	Yes	No	Yes
Losses allowed on owner's taxes	Yes	Yes	Yes	No	Yes

election has lost its effectiveness before the maximum of 35 stockholders has been reached, and the company will want to rescind this status. For those early years of a growth company, or for the entire life of a reasonably small and closely held company, S corporation status can mean substantial tax savings to the company and its owners.

Conclusion: Advantages/Disadvantages of Each Form

Table 3–1 summarizes the principal advantages and disadvantages of each of the major business forms available to the entrepreneur. The decision about which form of business is best for you is too important to be made without first consulting an attorney and an accountant. The most common preference is for the corporation, whether in the normal or the S corporation form. Your unique circumstances may be such, though, that some other type of business form would be preferable. Armed with the knowledge of your options and informed by the advice of professionals, you can make the best decision for *your* needs.

CHAPTER 4

RAISING MONEY
FOR YOUR BUSINESS

Proven strategies and techniques for dealing with investors

In This Chapter:

1. Where to find money for your business
2. Types of investors identified, explained, and ranked:
   a. Banks
   b. Venture Capital Companies
   c. Small Business Investment Companies (SBICs)
   d. Investment Bankers, Stockbrokers
   e. Small Business Administration (SBA)
   f. Private Investors
3. How to deal with investors and what to say to them
4. Legal issues: Business Plan vs. Offering Memorandum
5. Closing the deal: Meeting the potential investors
6. How much of the company to offer investors
7. Should you issue stocks, bonds, or convertible securities?

WHERE TO FIND MONEY FOR YOUR BUSINESS

The business press frequently carries reports of entrepreneurs who have raised millions of dollars through venture capitalists or initial public offerings (IPOs). Other entrepreneurs see these highly publicized success stories and ask, "Where is *our* money?" If there are so many investors around, why are they so hard to find? One problem is that the press only reports the success stories—it wouldn't make very exciting news to report about *failures* to raise capital—and they leave out all the details about how the successful parties achieved their goals.

A prestigious national business publication recently began what was to be a series of features examining the common problems faced by business. The series was supposed to analyze business failures and give insight into the reasons for such failures. The series was to have included articles on unsuccessful searches for funding. A curious thing happened, though. After the first article in the series appeared, that initial concept was abandoned by the editors. It seems that the readers didn't want to hear about business failures and problems. Their prime interest was in the glamour of success stories.

Venture capitalist Arthur Rock, writing in the *Harvard Business Review,* estimates that he sees about 300 business plans a year. Of these, he supplies capital to one or two. What happens to the other 298? They are never heard about in the press. The one or two companies which *were* funded go on to success, and initial public offerings often make the founders wealthy. We read about these successes in books, magazines, and newspapers, and we see features about them on television.

For most of us, then, the odds of receiving funding from a venture capitalist are probably less than 1 percent; financing must be found elsewhere. This is the real dilemma the businessperson faces, and it's one which should be addressed directly and candidly.

Your Own Money

If you have the liquid capital necessary to finance your own business, and you are willing to risk it on your venture, you are in an ideal position: You won't have to answer to anyone but yourself. Investors will not have any ownership or secured interest in your operations, so they won't be looking over your shoulder. Banks will not press you for costly regular financial statements or restrict your spending habits. You will truly be your own boss.

Few people, of course, can finance their business themselves. Most have to look to outside sources to finance at least a portion of their capital needs, especially if any appreciable growth is planned. There is even a school of thought which says that the risk inherent in a new business venture should always be shared, regardless of how much money the entrepreneur has available for personal investment. This school believes that the entrepreneur will make wiser and more reasonable decisions when other parties are at risk in the business, and that the opinions and input of these outside investors can be valuable. Yet, the decision is rightfully yours when it comes to the amount of personal funds you want to invest in your business. There are tradeoffs, but we recommend that you read this section before making a decision on the amount of personal funds you plan to use in capitalizing your business.

Personal Borrowing
Transferring cash from personal savings into a business is not the only method of funding a business. Cash can be raised by establishing a line of credit at a bank, and borrowing against personal assets. A lender will examine your personal assets and your credit history and will make a decision based on these criteria. Assuming you are a good credit risk, the bank won't place a great deal of emphasis on what you plan to do with the money.

Bankers will be most interested in the assets offered as security. A major qualification for these assets is a lasting value and a relative liquidity. Real estate, blue-chip stocks, high-quality bonds, and certificates of deposit are examples of personal assets that can be offered as security. The future, projected earnings of a business are rarely viewed as a lendable asset by a banker.

When you borrow money personally to invest in a business, one of the best ways to transfer the funds is by lending your money to the company on the same terms as you received it from the bank. The business then tries to make the payments with its cashflow. If there is a period of time during which the company does not have a regular cashflow, negotiate with the lender for a similar period of time during which no payments will be required on the loan. These terms can be arranged with all but the most rigid of bankers.

Negotiating with Banks

How many times have you seen a person happily entering a bank to borrow money? Not often, probably. It seems that most borrowers approach their bankers with apprehension. A Midwest businessman we know approaches his banks in an unusual, but successful, manner. He doesn't use the standard bank loan request forms and financial questionnaires they provide. Instead, he prepares a package of information which includes:

- A market study which details his assessment of his industry, competition, the strengths and weaknesses of both his company and his competitions', and his plans for maintaining and then increasing his market share for the next five years.
- An economic scenario that he envisions will occur, along with a best case and worst case strategy for reacting to that scenario.
- An updated version of his business plan's main changes over the past three years (an indication that he can react to change) with notations explaining the strategy behind the changes.
- Two versions of his financial statements. The first prepared in standard form by his accountants, and the second clearly showing how the statements would look if he were not taking his high personal expenses (cars, expenses, travel, and other "perks" that can be hidden in financial statements).
- An organizational chart with detailed resumes of his key people. Also noted are his plans to add personnel over the next five years to provide for projected growth.
- His personal financial statement, which is obviously understated.
- A projected cash flow statement that illustrates three dif-

ferent loan amounts and how they will be repaid over a period of time. The amount he actually wants to borrow is the lowest of the three.

He then presents this package to each banker personally and carefully explains the documents, section by section. In this way, he has anticipated the banker's questions and concerns, and has made him feel fully at ease. Before the meeting ends, he asks the banker to prepare a proposal for him to consider. The businessman also tells the banker that she is one of three lending institutions that are competing for this business; and he parts company with the lending officer by mentioning a deadline for the proposal—usually around ten to fifteen days.

This method works splendidly for this particular businessman. It may not be as applicable for a new venture or a struggling business, but it shows that *banks will negotiate*. Look at it like this: A borrower "rents" the use of the bank's money; this makes the borrower a customer, with the right to negotiate for the best deal.

The Lone Entrepreneur
If you take money out of savings to capitalize your business, or sell assets to raise cash, or borrow the money personally and invest it into the business, the buck still stops with you. Are you ready for this? Or would you rather share the risk, and at the same time the decision making, the rewards, and the glory (or ridicule)? If you would prefer to share the risk, or if you don't have the capability to capitalize the business yourself, you will have to prepare yourself for the search for *OPM*.

Other People's Money (OPM)

You may have heard the term OPM in the press. Many entrepreneurs say their success has been based on their ability to use OPM—"Other People's Money." Of course, the rewards must then be shared with these other people, but the risk is shared as well.

The key point for the entrepreneur to realize is that the risks and the rewards do not necessarily have to be shared proportionately when OPM is used.

As an example, let's say you need $200,000 to capitalize your business. You put up $25,000 and are looking for investors for the rest. You propose that 25 percent of the stock of the company be reserved for the investors, while you keep the balance of 75 percent. Now, anyone knows that $25,000 is not 75 percent of $200,000 (it is only 12.5 percent). But we don't have to show equal proportions because we're talking about two different types of stockholders—an "active" one (you), and "passive" ones (the investors).

You deserve a greater amount of stock because you're putting in "sweat equity." Sweat equity is the total value of (1) your ideas, (2) the research you've done, (3) the time it's taken to put the project together, and (4) the special qualities you bring to the table as organizer, promoter, chief executive, and general manager.

Is it fair to offer investors a share of stock for $10 when you bought the same stock for one penny plus sweat equity? Of course it's fair, and it's done all the time. Just read the prospectus of any initial public stock offering. You'll see what the original owners paid for their stock in relation to what the public is being asked to pay. There are precedents everywhere for this seemingly lopsided equity distribution. And they all have one thing in common: *The price of the stock sold to investors in an offering is almost always based on the **future** earnings of the venture.*

Expect to Negotiate with Investors

You need to realize that sophisticated investors will negotiate with you to determine the amount of stock they get for the price they pay. You should decide early on in your efforts to raise money whether or not you are willing to negotiate price or percentage with potential investors. Fairness should be shown to all the investors who participate within the same time period; and if a reduced price or larger percentage is negotiated for one, then you should readjust all the other investments made at the same time.

The best approach to take when raising money is to make sure that the proposal is a good deal for everyone involved. Don't try to overvalue your company or overprice your stock. In this way you'll be able to return to the same investors in the future for additional capital, should you need it. Treat your investors with fairness, respect, and courtesy. Keep them apprised of what is going on in your business, both the good and the bad, and they will most likely stand behind you no matter how the company performs.

Where to Get OPM
Before you give much thought to whom you will approach for money, you should prepare a written business plan. We recommend that you make no attempt to discuss your proposition with anyone until you have finalized your plan. (Chapter Two explains in detail how to complete that business plan.) Without the plan, all your words are just so much hot air. We cannot stress this point enough:

> Your chances of raising money *with* a business plan are *many times* greater than your chances without one.

In fact, if the investors you approach are sophisticated and experienced, your chances of success in raising money without a business plan are virtually nil.

TYPES OF INVESTORS

Once the business plan is completed, you must decide which types of investors will be approached. Who are these investors, and what are their characteristics? Which are most likely to respond favorably to your particular proposal? We'll help you target those who are most apt to invest in your venture, and warn you about those who will probably have little interest.

In the following section, we discuss the various types of investors and rank them according to their likelihood of showing an interest in your new venture. These rankings are based on solid experience, and will be on a scale of 1 to 10 (10 being the highest probability, and 1 the lowest). Remember, of course, that a number of factors affect your chances of success in raising money, from the quality of your idea and your background to the state of the economy in general.

Banks

Banks are in the business of renting money, not trading it for something of indeterminate value, like stock in a startup company. Banks are also subject to state and federal regulations, which often prohibit them from investing in high-risk endeavors. Venture capital, as a rule, is taboo for banks. Don't even bother to approach your friendly local banker with an offer of an equity position in your company. If you need to *borrow* money, the banker is the logical one to visit. As a prospective *investor*, though, the bank is not one of your options. (Also see *SBA.)*

BANKS
Ranking: 1

Venture Capital Companies

Venture capitalists are *the* professional high-risk investors. Their job is to invest money in new or emerging companies or in the buyout of proven existing companies. These investors acknowledge the high-risk nature of the investments, so they closely scrutinize potential new investments.

The Management Team Is Critical
Experience has taught venture capitalists that the best chance for success comes when a company is run by a well-rounded management team. Ideally, this team has either prospered in a similar type of venture, or has many years of experience and achievement in business. Experience is important. The venture capital industry has a saying, "It is better to have first-rate managers with a second-rate product than second-rate managers with a first-rate product."

Venture capitalists know that first-rate founders increase the chances for the success of a new venture. One of their strictest requirements is that you have a sharp, experienced management team. If you plan to manage your business and do not have a successful startup or business experience in your past, your chances of finding investment dollars at the venture capitalist's table are very poor.

Herd Instinct

Venture capitalists also seem to follow what is called the "herd instinct." They like their investments to follow a pattern which has been set by other venture capitalists. Very few are willing to risk making investments in industries that are currently not in vogue. The favored industries go in and out of vogue all the time. At one time it might be medical service companies, and six months later computer software firms. But if you're not in one of these "hot" industries, your chances with the venture capitalists will be slim.

Minimum Requirements

Venture capitalists require significant "upside potential" for their investments. "Upside potential" means that the sales and profits should have enough potential to offer investors tremendous financial returns. Sufficient sales and profits are considered to be projected sales of at least $25 million or $35 million by the fifth year, and profits of 5 to 10 percent on those sales. Numbers below this threshold will leave a venture capitalist cold.

The venture capitalists want a return of 5 to 10 times their investment in about five years. They also tend to limit their minimum investment to $100,000 in any company. Investments of less than $250,000 are considered unattractive. Venture capitalists take this position because they must spend approximately the same amount of time on each company in their portfolio. As a result, they don't want to take valuable time away from a $500,000 investment to spend on a $100,000 one.

High Risk, High Reward

Venture capital failures must be offset by the performance of the other companies in their portfolio. Knowing that perhaps 10 to 20 percent of their investments will go sour, venture capitalists aim high to achieve a respectable level of performance for *their* investors. The venture capital pools are almost always funded by a number of large institutional investors—pension funds, major corporations, insurance companies, or wealthy families—and the venture capitalist is directly accountable to those investors.

If you are predicting significant growth for your company—along the lines described above—and have a well-prepared business plan and a core group of experienced managers, you might do well with this highly selective group of investors.

VENTURE CAPITALISTS
Ranking: 3–4

Small Business Investment Companies (SBICs)

Many people in the investment community incorrectly group SBICs into the same category as the venture capital companies. For the most part, SBICs are a distinct group, with their own characteristics. It's important to understand these important differences.

Some SBICs are similar to venture capital companies, having the same stringent requirements for their investments—experienced management and large numbers. But these SBICs are the exception rather than the rule. The majority are privately held companies (not publicly traded on the stock exchanges), and are relatively small when compared to venture capital companies. Managers of most SBICs are less sophisticated and somewhat less demanding than the managing partners of the venture capital firms. For this reason alone, SBICs are more likely to react favorably to a well planned and clearly presented business venture from a less experienced entrepreneur.

The Best Approach
The best approach to use with SBICs is to first do some research on their preferences and background. Learn about the types of businesses that are preferred, and which type and size investment seems to be the norm. You can find this information at your local library's reference section. The following points will be useful in conducting such research:

1. Get the most recent information available on the total capital of each SBIC in your area.

2. Find the funds those SBICs currently have available for investment.
3. Determine the average size of their investments.
4. Learn whether they prefer to buy stock in their portfolio companies or to lend them money.
5. Learn who the people are who run the SBIC, and what type of industries they favor.

By gathering this information, you can approach the SBICs that are most likely to be favorable to your proposal, and you can give them what they want. If approached in a professional, businesslike manner, and with a proposal that matches their preferred size and type of investment, most SBICs will be quite receptive.

SBICs
Ranking: 6–8

Investment Bankers (Brokerage Firms)

The term "investment banker" generally refers to an individual or firm that procures capital for companies in need of financing. An investment banker usually acts as an agent (broker) or adviser for that client company.

Selecting an Investment Banker
The major investment bankers seldom look for startup or early stage companies. They prefer to spend their time raising money for more established companies. But there are certain investment bankers, firms much smaller than the Merrill Lynches, that may be responsive to your proposal. Their degree of interest will depend upon a number of factors, such as

1. Current state of the economy.
2. Strength of the stock market.
3. Investor appetite for new issues.
4. The particular investment banker's ability to raise modest amounts of capital through "private placements"

(which are exempt from securities registration) and public stock offerings.

Besides these, two other factors will affect their interest in your proposal: How easy your company's stock would be to sell to investors, and the long-term potential for your company's success.

The Investment Banker as Salesman
These last two factors are easier to understand if you realize how an investment banker/broker works in relation to the stock market. The broker's job is to *sell* investments to clients. If he doesn't sell, he doesn't make any money; and he is in business to make money. Your company should be presented as an *easy sale*. To excite the interest of investors, your company should have aggressive but realistic plans, good management, and be in an industry or niche that is growing. Preferably, it should be in an industry that is currently an investment favorite. It should be clear that your company's chances for success are very high.

Winners Only Need Apply
As a professional, the investment banker wants to be associated with winners. He wants to see his clients' investments increase in value. And of course, pointing to his or her successful stock selections of the past makes the broker's job—selling stock—easier.

The broker often profits in another way when the companies he has backed have done well; he profits by selling stock warrants obtained when the company went public. If your business plan describes a company whose prospects are nearly surefire, there is a strong opportunity to obtain the funding through a local or regional investment banker.

Timing Is Critical
The real estate industry has a saying that you've probably heard, that the three most important things in real estate are "Location, location, and location." Similarly, the three most

important things in trying to raise capital for your business through investment bankers are "Timing, timing, and timing." Even if your project is a good one, if the economy and the stock market are in a recession, this avenue of financing will be extremely tight with its resources. On the other hand, if stock market investors are eager to buy new issues of companies with little or no operating history, *then* your timing can be perfect; and you should start approaching investment bankers immediately.

INVESTMENT BANKERS
Ranking (if market timing is good): 7–9
Ranking (if the market is bad): 0–3

Small Business Administration (SBA)

The Small Business Administration was established to help small and medium-sized businesses in the United States by offering loan guarantee programs, direct loans, and various advisory and assistance functions. An important objective of the SBA has been the creation of new jobs, especially in economically depressed areas. The political logic was to help small business through loans and loan guarantees and thus to produce more jobs.

Not a Give-away Program
How can you obtain money through the SBA? First, it is important to realize that the SBA is not in the business of simply giving away money. Your venture must make good economic sense, and it must be presented in an organized and professional manner.

Second, most of the funding that's available from the SBA is actually in the form of bank loans that are guaranteed by the SBA. A company must be turned down for normal financing by at least three banks, after which it can apply for a loan through what is called a "participating" bank, one which is a participant in the SBA program. The participating bank presents the company's application to the SBA. If approved, the SBA guarantees up to 90 percent of the loan.

Political Football

The SBA loan guarantee program has been kicked back and forth among politicians over the past decade; various factions have fought over the amount of funding it should receive. At the time of publication, the program has been pruned to a very minimal level. Getting SBA assistance on a loan today is difficult. This situation could change quickly, however, and the program could once again be funded as in the past.

Initial Steps

The easiest way to find out about the current status of the SBA program, and which banks in your area are participating banks, is to ask the nearest SBA office. The office can be found in your telephone directory under "United States Government." Your local SBA office can provide you with the necessary forms, including filing instructions. Although their information package will probably not mention it, your chances of success with the SBA will be greatly enhanced if your application contains a complete business plan.

Intelligence Gathering

Call several participating banks and talk to the loan officer in charge of SBA loans. Explain to the officer that you are interested in the SBA guaranteed loan program. Set up a meeting to discuss SBA requirements and procedures. Ask the officer what kind of loans—size, terms, and type of business— the bank typically makes. Determine the amount of assistance the bank is willing to provide in completing the SBA application package.

Don't come to the *first* meeting loaded down with business plans, financial statements, and other paperwork. The first objectives are to *gather general information* about what the bank will require for your *next* meeting and to be sure that the bank is interested enough in your general plan to work with you. Once you know the kind of specific information your banker wants, give it to him or her with the initial application. Tailoring the proposal to the bank's requirements will greatly increase your chances of a favorable response.

Collateral and Personal Guarantees

Almost inevitably, you will be required to give a personal guarantee on an SBA-backed loan. Assets—probably both personal and business assets—will be required as collateral for the loan. These loans are not gifts. The government expects repayment, and they've gotten tough about this.

SMALL BUSINESS ADMINISTRATION
Ranking: 5–6

Private Investors

Now we'll discuss everyone's favorite source of investment capital: the private investor! Probably 98 percent of the new ventures in America are financed by private investors. They are your best resource for funding, especially when it comes to initial capital.

A Typical Scenario

Let's take an example: You are the average American, having worked as an employee for someone else for all of your working life. You have built up a reasonable nest egg, but you've had little if any chance to get really rich. All this time, you've been exposed to entrepreneurial success stories, like those of Apple Computers, Federal Express, and Domino's Pizza. You've naturally felt that opportunities such as these had passed you by.

Then an impressive entrepreneur asks if you would invest in his new venture. The business plan is extremely sound; the product or service a natural moneymaker. The deal offers you a return of many times your investment if the projected goals are met. Your investment will not expose your financial security to undue risk.

Imagine that the entrepreneur is someone who came to you highly recommended by your attorney or your accountant, or by a businessman whose opinion you respect. Perhaps you were introduced to this entrepreneur by a friend who is already an investor. Given all of these factors, you might decide to say yes to this opportunity.

Is this scenario unrealistic? Not at all! It frequently happens, and can be reality for you and your investors.

The Image of Success Defined

Think for a moment about that fictitious entrepreneur we just created. Get a picture fixed in your mind of this successful person. We described the person as *impressive*. What is an *impressive* person in your mind? It's likely that the image is of someone dressed in a business suit, well-groomed; an articulate speaker with a high degree of confidence. This person has produced a dynamic business plan containing all the answers to a host of business and financial questions.

Is the description of this person close to your image of the successful entrepreneur? Probably so. There are certain things present in most successful people, and some of these qualities are easily identified: *businesslike, well-groomed, confident,* and *very informed.* Potential investors will expect such traits in *you* if they are to put money in your hands.

"Playing the part"—creating the physical presence of a successful person—is a psychological advantage that is yours for the taking. It is a positive step towards obtaining the money that you need to start your business. Look the part, and you will have given yourself another advantage, one that may be critical to your financing efforts.

The Best People to Approach

Who are the best people to approach as potential investors? Initially, those that know you well and have the most positive feelings toward you, are the best. Even if you don't get the funding you need from these people, you will gain experience in making your presentation and develop confidence by starting with them. In any case, your chances of success are probably best with this group.

If Uncle John has always thought of you as bright and a hard worker, someone destined to go far, then by all means ask Uncle John to invest in your venture. But don't be offended if he is unwilling to invest—he may have personal reasons for not doing so. Be sure to ask him for the names of others who might be interested in investing in your venture.

How to Approach Potential Investors
Make a list of all the people you know who think enough of you to possibly to take a gamble on your venture. But when you approach these people, whether they're relatives or acquaintances, don't do it casually. *Treat the whole situation as a business affair.* Pick a businesslike environment in which to meet and discuss your project, and establish an appointed time in advance.

When you *do* make your presentation, don't expect an answer right away. Give the investor some time to digest the material and your proposal, and set a date to get back in touch with them about it—to answer any questions they might have. Set a cut-off date after which you will not accept any more investors, and include the date in your business plan and any other material you prepare. (Some investment offerings include a sliding scale for the cost of stock, so that early investors are rewarded for their prompt action). Be sure to ask each of these potential investors for names of other people who might be interested in your project. Don't be shy about it. After all, you're only doing your job as an entrepreneur.

Referrals
Hopefully, you will have used a CPA when you put together your financial projections. That CPA can now be the source of some excellent referrals. Ask them to contact some of their clients who might be interested in your venture. Check with your attorney for similar referrals. The key here is *persistence.*

Perhaps the best source of referrals is your *stockbroker.* (He or she might even invest in your venture.) Stockbrokers are, by nature, speculators. They have seen so many deals become big winners that they are always looking for opportunities of their own.

Brokers talk among themselves constantly. When you convince *one* stockbroker to invest, several others tag along. You may find a broker who will convince a few of his clients to invest in your venture. Get your stockbroker excited about your company, invite him to invest, and ask for referrals.

The Best Source of Capital

The private investor is the best source of investment capital. They are far better than the investment banker, the SBIC or the professional venture capital firm. Approach private investors carefully and with a highly polished presentation. *Prepare and present a business plan!* Then ask them to invest. Regardless of their answer, be sure to get some referrals.

PRIVATE INVESTORS
Ranking: 9–10

DEALING WITH POTENTIAL INVESTORS: PREPARE, PREPARE, PREPARE

It is not uncommon to see an entrepreneur throw a presentation together (possibly not even on paper) and expect investors to trample each other on the way to invest in the new venture.

Investors do not share the special vision that is the driving force behind the entrepreneur. Your ideas, unless supported by facts and reasonable assumptions, will not be embraced by investors and lenders. But they are more likely to share your vision and dreams if certain steps are taken—steps which appeal to the psyche of the targeted investor or lender. These steps represent advantages that are essential to winning the enthusiasm of others. A good entrepreneur will always develop every advantage which is available.

Treat Investors with Care

Think of an investor as the most important person in the world. They have a busy schedule and will only talk to you *once. There is no second chance.* Convince yourself that it is earthshakingly important to get that person to invest money in your venture. In this frame of mind, you certainly won't want to offend or alienate the potential investor in any way.

You know, for instance, that he prefers his hair short and wears gray conservative three-piece suits. Give him the impression that you are like him. Arrive for your meeting with short hair and a gray three-piece suit. You may not convince him that he should invest just because of your appearance, but it's better than starting off on the wrong foot by appearing at his office with disheveled hair and dressed in casual clothes. His thinking might very well be that *he's* successful, and that all the other successful people he knows dress like he does. *You* dress differently, therefore you will *not* be successful.

He may not consciously experience these feelings, but they'll be there subconsciously. Certainly, this rationale is totally faulty, but *you'll* be wrong if you think his feelings, subconscious or otherwise, won't affect your chances at getting his financial support.

The "No Socks" Episode

We once participated in a meeting where two experienced and articulate young real estate promoters made a presentation to the top officers of an investment banking firm. The promoters were seeking funding to develop an exciting resort property on the west coast of Florida. The presentation was very professional, and the overall deal was financially sound. But when the two promoters left the investment bankers' office, the first reaction from the president of the investment firm was, "Did you see that? They weren't wearing socks!"

This one faux pas killed any chance the promoters had of obtaining financing from the investment bankers. The project may have been a profitable one for the investment bankers. It certainly had the potential. But these Wall Street professionals were not going to finance any real estate development run by people who *didn't wear socks!*

Know Your Material

Being well-prepared when making your presentation is the biggest advantage you can give yourself. Do your research. Know your market and your competition. Have a thorough and well-written business plan. And go a couple of steps further: Find out as much as possible about your potential investors. Review their previous investments and ventures.

Knowing your investor as an individual makes a positive impression. Build an information file. Ask questions beforehand, and then do some research on your own. Having knowledge and understanding of the investor's concerns, objectives, and past investments will provide great insight about how to approach this particular person. For the moment, this prospective investor *is* your "market," your "customer." Learn what he wants; then give it to him.

What to Bring to the First Meeting

Two items are essential at the first meeting with every potential investor: your business plan and a written investment purchase agreement ("stock subscription agreement"). The business plan is your sales material, the tangible evidence of your intangible ideas. Without it, your business idea has no substance. The subscription agreement will allow the investor to actually make an investment when the time comes.

The subscription agreement should be prepared by an attorney experienced in securities law. "Legal form" books contain samples of these agreements for you to follow, but that route exposes you to the risk of overlooking important considerations. Be sure the agreement is properly prepared by having a competent professional do the work for you.

LEGAL DISCLOSURES AND OFFERING MEMORANDUMS

The subscription agreement should not be part of the business plan itself. If the agreement is included in the body of the plan, the package can be construed to be an "offering circular." An offering circular is a formal document of disclosure, similar in content to a registration statement, which is provided to investors for offerings that are exempt from SEC registration requirements. Various laws apply to offering circulars, and it's best if you can avoid unnecessary filings with the many agencies that regulate securities.

The Attorneys' Viewpoint

Many, if not most, attorneys specializing in securities law are very cautious in their interpretation of the laws governing registration of "securities." They will usually insist that a detailed (and expensive) Memorandum be prepared if you plan on raising money from private investors. An Offering Memorandum contains many of the same disclosures found in a public offering and warns investors of the potential high risk involved in the investment. If you have the opportunity to read a memorandum, do so; it may lead you to wonder how *anyone* is ever successful in raising money with such negative material.

The major risk encountered by not preparing an Offering Memorandum is that—in the event your venture fails—you could be held personally liable for the losses of the investors. Despite this potential risk, these elaborate and expensive documents are usually unnecessary. As an illustration of this point, one of the authors conducted an informal poll of venture capital firms and investment bankers for their views on this subject.

The author was participating as a principal in a startup which was seeking approximately one million dollars in initial capital. A business plan had been prepared. Legal and accounting relationships were being established. A large regional law firm recommended that an Offering Memorandum be prepared before any attempts were made to raise money. The author did not agree with this approach, maintaining that an Offering Memorandum was an unnecessary waste of time and money (about $35,000).

Disagreeing with the attorneys, the author proceeded to conduct a phone survey of professional venture capital investors. Each professional was asked about his thoughts on Offering Memorandums for companies that approached them for financing. They were also asked how many of their investments originally included an Offering Memorandum. Without exception, the venture capitalists confirmed our opinion. *None* of the companies that received their financial backing had presented a formal Offering Memorandum.

Several of these venture capitalists even commented that

it would be insulting to see a proposal presented to them in the form of an Offering Memorandum, as if to imply a lack of sophistication in determining the risks, the validity of the facts, and the reasonableness of the financial forecasts. To some, a Memorandum was a sure sign that the proposal was being shopped around and shown indiscriminately to anyone who would look at it, in a shotgun approach to finding an investor. This approach is the kiss of death when dealing with venture capitalists.

The startup company proceeded to raise capital without the use of an Offering Memorandum, and no problems developed as a result of this decision.

Which Document to Use

If you are planning to raise money only from family and friends, from professional venture capitalists, or investment bankers, then it's safe to proceed without a formal Offering Memorandum. On the other hand, if you approach the general public with your package—people whom you've never met before—then an Offering Memorandum may be required. Use a combination of common sense and professional legal advice to reach a decision on this matter. Just remember that you can be sued at any time for almost anything, so don't let the potential for personal financial liability intimidate you into spending thousands of dollars that might be better spent elsewhere. The decision is ultimately yours, and not your attorney's.

MEETING WITH THE POTENTIAL INVESTORS

Preparation for the First Meeting

Prior to the meeting, write down the most important and exciting points about your venture. Arrange these key points in logical order. Tie them together with clearly marked indicators on the pages of the business plan. Then practice the entire presentation in the privacy of your home or office.

Time yourself, if you feel the need. Be sure the presentation doesn't evolve into a fixed speech. What you say should be spontaneous and spoken from the heart, instead of by rote. Sometimes it's helpful to use a tape or video recorder to play back your presentation for self-criticism. Did you cover all the points and sound confident and professional? Did you refer to the appropriate sections of the business plan as you spoke, so that a listener could tell that what you were saying was magnified in greater detail in the written material?

Your First Meeting

Come to the meeting with the specific purpose of explaining your venture. Remember, your goal is to make a favorable impression the *first* time. Sell *yourself,* not the investment. Bring your business plan and go through it with the investor. Show him or her which sections of the business plan summarize your unique concept, and simply refer to these sections as you describe your ideas. Don't read anything word for word. Your presentation shouldn't be more than 15 or 20 minutes. It's important not to confuse and overwhelm the listener with too much detail. Concentrate on the main points and leave the minutiae to the business plan or to a later meeting.

Interruptions Work to Your Advantage

During the actual presentation to an investor, you will be interrupted occasionally with questions. Welcome these interruptions, for they show that the investor is interested. If possible, answer the investor by referring him to a particular part of the business plan. It adds to your credibility when you can say, "We've researched that, and the statistics show . . . You'll find the research on page [ ] in the Appendix." It's important to have answered the investor's question, but it's equally important to show that the information and all the supporting data is already present in the business plan. This emphasizes that you've done your homework, and adds credibility to your presentation.

Accurate Answers Are an Asset

A ready access to pertinent facts that result in credibility is the main reason to do all or most of the research for your business plan yourself. The investor wants *you* to know the important facts, not a consultant who was hired to write the business plan. When asked pertinent questions, you must be able to answer quickly and with confidence. It's always possible, of course, that you'll be asked something for which you don't have an answer. In that case, simply say "That's something I can't answer right now, but it's a good point and I'm glad you brought it up. I'll spend some time researching it and get you an answer."

It may not be necessary to get the investor his answer before he makes a decision, but you should follow through on your commitment to look into the matter. Be sure to write the question down as soon as you leave the meeting—don't trust your memory. The investor is bound to be impressed by your personal organization if you get an answer back to him quickly.

Ending the Meeting

At the end of the meeting, leave a copy of the business plan with the investor. Give him the subscription agreement in a separate folder. Tell him you'll call next week to discuss the proposition.

Follow-up

Take the initiative and contact the prospective investor by phone within five to seven days after the meeting. If he is not available when you call, do not ask that he return the call. Ask when it would be best to reach him. Stay in control of the situation. Don't get caught playing "phone tag."

When you reach the potential investor, ask him outright, "Have you had enough time to make a decision?" If the answer is yes, simply ask what amount he has decided to invest. If the answer is no, attempt to learn exactly what needs to be done in order for him to reach a decision. Be specific in your questions. Don't let indecision drag on. Consider using a deadline beyond which it will be impossible to accept him as an investor. Most people need this little nudge, so use it unless it is entirely inappropriate.

For investors who say yes, ask that the subscription agreement be completed and returned with a check as soon as possible. Prompt them to immediate action.

HOW MUCH OF THE COMPANY SHOULD BE OFFERED TO INVESTORS?

The methods and procedures for establishing the value of a company are well-known to professional venture capitalists and investment bankers. Why have these procedures remained "secret" for so many years? We don't know the answer to that question, but we intend to open the door and share these valuable secrets.

Where To Start

The initial step involves establishing a *specific value* for your company at a given future date. This may seem almost impossible for a startup company, but it's easier than it seems. You simply assume that the company will perform exactly as you have predicted in your financial projections. You know how much you've projected the company will be making in profits, so the company's future financial condition can be readily calculated.

Select a Year

What's the appropriate future time frame for the valuation? Five years should be your mark for valuation. Why? Simply because the five-year mark is used by the majority of professionals in the investment field. It has become a common denominator. By using the same point in time, your valuation will approximate that of the professionals.

The Six Steps to Valuation (Note: Financial Statements Are Essential to These Steps!)

1. Your business plan has a section on "Financials," which includes a five-year projection of income (the "Forecasted Financial Statements"). This projection shows the expected profitability of your company for each of its five initial years. The figure needed for this exercise is the *Net After-Tax Income* for the *fifth year*. Don't use the combined Net Income of the first five years, or the average Net Income over the first five years. Your fifth year Net After-Tax Income should be clearly indicated on the financial statements.

2. Next, find several publicly traded companies similar to your own, or companies that resemble what your company should be in five years. Compare the type of industry, business specialty, geographic location, size, and annual growth rate. You probably know some of these companies as a result of your own industry research. *Find the Price-Earnings Multiples* of these companies, either by checking the stock market listings in the Wall Street Journal or by asking your broker. The Price-Earnings Multiple is commonly referred to as the P/E Ratio. This number represents the company's current market price divided by its per-share net income.

As an example, if a company had net income of $1,000,000 in its most recent year and it had 100,000 shares of stock in existence, then its per-share earnings would be $10. If the stock sold for $200 per share at the present time, then its P/E Ratio would be 20 ($200 / $10).

The P/E Ratio is a good indicator of what the market thinks the company is worth. Since this ratio is probably the most widely accepted method of measuring the relative value of a company, it is the one you should use.

3. Calculate the average P/E Ratio for the public companies that will act as your benchmarks. Multiply that number (the average P/E Ratio of the companies) by the net income for your fifth year of operations. *The resulting amount is the estimated value of your company at the end of its fifth year of operations* (assuming that it performs as you have projected in the Forecasted Financial Statements). It's not the value of the business *today,* or next year, but the value at a point five years from now. Of course, everyone realizes that your net income will probably turn out differently than you've projected. But all you're trying to do is establish the most *reasonable* estimate of the future value of the company.

4. For the moment, set aside the valuation arrived at in step 3. Next, select an *objective for your investors.* How much do they expect to earn for every dollar they invested? Obviously, each investor will have somewhat varied expectations. Most of the *professionals*—the venture capitalists and the investment bankers—expect a return between five and ten times their original investment in five years. A reasonable number to work with is probably *seven* times their investment in five years.

If your investor is not experienced, explain this process to him. He probably will want as much as the professionals will receive. Take the initiative and suggest that seven times his money is a considerable return. Guide him to this objective. It is a very generous goal and is usually much higher than his own personal projections.

5. Assuming your investor wants to earn seven dollars for every dollar invested, let's go back to the Financial section of the business plan. This time the objective will be to find the total amount that must initially be raised to capitalize the venture. (This isn't the amount you will need to get you through the entire next five years, but only what's required to launch the business). This amount should be the "total" on the Use of Proceeds Statement. Take this amount—let's say it's $100,000— and multiply it by seven (as in "seven times their investment in five years"). This will give you the total value the investors will look for at the end of five years. In our example, it would be $700,000 (7 times $100,000).

6. You now have the estimated value of the company (the estimated net income in year five multiplied by the P/E ratio). You also have established the return that will satisfy your investors after five years. All that remains is to determine the percentage of the company that should be offered to the investor that will yield the desired return. You can identify the correct percentage by dividing the amount of the investor's desired value by the estimated future value of the company.

If we assume that our company is projecting net income for its fifth year in the amount of $280,000, and the average P/E ratio for similar public companies is 10, then the estimated value of the company at the end of year five will be $2,800,000. Dividing the $700,000 desired investor's return by the $2,800,000 value of the company, we arrive at 25 percent. So, the amount of the company offered to the investor should be 25 percent of the total issued stock. If you were issuing 10,000 shares, then 2,500 shares would be offered for the startup capital you need.

Reasonably simple, isn't it? Yet this is one of the most difficult areas for most fledgling entrepreneurs (and some not-so-fledgling ones) to calculate.

Here is a summary of the above steps.

1. Determine the projected net income for the fifth year of operations from the five-year projections.
2. Find the average Price-Earnings Multiple of publicly held companies similar to your own.
3. Multiply the amounts from steps 1 and 2 together to arrive at the estimated value of your company in five years.
4. Select an investment objective for your investor. Start with a return of *seven* times their money.
5. Multiply the amount of startup capital needed (from the Use of Proceeds statement) by the investor's objective (*seven* times their investment) in step 4.
6. Divide the fifth year value of their dollars the investors should expect (Step 5) by the estimated value of the company (Step 3). Multiply this factor (a percentage) times the total number of shares issued, and you have the number of shares to offer to the investor.

Note: You can adjust the objective used in Step 4, using anything from five to seven, and get different percentages of the company. But any return above five (500 percent) in five years is a pretty good one. Be sure your investor understands this method of calculating return.

Table 4–1 presents an example of the valuation formula.

Investors' Expected Value Is Not "Cash"

These calculations do not mean that your investor necessarily "cashes out" at the end of five years. In fact, the investor may *never* realize the cash value of his investment unless the company is sold or "goes public." Unless an agreement exists to buy out the investor at a certain future date, the original investment simply remains in the company. The value of the company may increase, and the investor may even be able to borrow against this value. But he cannot expect a *cash* payout at the end of five years. The best analogy is an investment in real estate: When the real estate increases in *value* it doesn't result in the investor receiving actual cash equaling the increased value. In order for the investor to "cash out," the real estate must be sold, or the investor bought out by his partners.

What Happens If Actual Profits Are Different from Your Projections?

There is no "if" about it: Your actual profits *will* be different from your projections. It is only a matter of whether you will perform better or worse than projected. If your actual income varies by a large amount from what was projected, your investors will no doubt clearly express their reactions to you. Actual experience might present them with a return of two times their money rather than the five or seven times they had expected. What can be done about this potential problem? If your investor is concerned, there *is* a method "guaranteeing" his return, regardless of the negotiated rate of return.

Adjustable Percentages

You can base the investor's share of the company on the *actual* net income of the company in its fifth year. The mechanics

TABLE 4–1
The Six Steps to Valuation

Step #1

(From "Forecasted Income Statement")

	Year 5
Sales	$ 2,800,000
Cost of Sales	(1,120,000)
Gross Profit	1,680,000
Operating Expenses	(1,280,000)
Income (pre-tax)	400,000
Provision for Income Tax	(120,000)
Net Income (after tax)	$ 280,000[a]

[a] This is the figure to be used. It represents Net Income (after tax) for the fifth year of operations.

Step #2

Select several publicly traded companies that are similar to the company for which funds are being sought, and find their current P/E Ratios.

Examples:

Adams Design Corp.	P/E: 10
Smith Engineering, Inc.	P/E: 9
Brown Consulting	P/E: 11
Craft, Allen, & White, Inc.	P/E: 13
Williamson & Co., Inc.	P/E: 7

Step #3

The P/E ratios for the above companies are:

$$
\begin{array}{r}
10 \\
9 \\
11 \\
13 \\
\underline{7} \\
\underline{\underline{50}}
\end{array}
$$

The *average P/E* (50 divided by 5) is 10. 10 times $280,000 (see Step #1) = $2,800,000. $2,800,000 is the *estimated value of the company* after five years.

Step #4

Determine the *investors' objectives* for a return on their money. A reasonable return for this type of risk investment is *seven* times their investment in *five* years. An acceptable range is five to ten times their money in five years, but any specific number is negotiable.

TABLE 4–1—Continued

Step #5

Total Initial Capital sought from investors:
$100,000
Investors' objective—seven times this amount:
$700,000

Step #6

Investors' Objective:	$700,000
Estimated Value (5th yr.) of company	2,800,000

Divide "Investors' Objective total" by the "Estimated Value of Co." (700,000 by 2,800,00) = .25. 25 percent is a fair and reasonable portion of the Company's stock (in this example) to offer to investors for their investment totaling $100,000.

---

of making this adjustment are relatively simple and follow a logical process.

The investor is given a certain number of shares at the time of the initial investment. At the end of the fifth year, the investor's percentage of the company is adjusted to reflect the original projected return (five times his investment, or whatever you agreed upon). This is accomplished by issuing more shares according to a legal agreement drafted at the time the original investment is made.

This agreement should include at least the following provisions:

- An agreed-upon Price-Earnings Multiple. Don't attempt this agreement unless you first decide on a P/E to use for future valuation purposes. Without establishing a P/E multiple, conflicts may arise in the future regarding the fairness of the valuation process.
- An agreement on the amount of the investor's objective (five times, or seven times his investment, or ten times, etc.).
- The *type* of financial statement to be used in determining the net income in the fifth year. Will it be prepared by

a CPA? By a particular CPA? Will it be a "reviewed" statement, or an "audited" one? Audits cost you a good deal of money. If the investor insists upon one you should decide in advance who will bear the cost.
- An agreement on the *mechanics* of the stock transfer. Your attorney can assist with this.

How Adjustment Works

Let's look at an example of this equity adjustment formula. Assume that the investor is being asked to put in $250,000, and that the current projections for the company show net income in the fifth year of $350,000. The Price-Earnings ratio decided upon is 14. (This scenario is different from the previous example.)

	As Projected	Actual
Fifth Year Net Income	$350,000	$300,000
P/E Ratio	14	14
Value of Company in Future	$4,900,000	$4,200,000
Investor's Objective (7 × $250,000)	$1,750,000	$1,750,000
Percentage of Equity	35%	42%

In this example, 35 percent of the company stock was originally issued to the investor. After five years, the company's net income is less than had been projected, so its valuation is also below original projections. The investor receives an additional seven percent of the stock, presumably out of the authorized but unissued shares, to bring the total up to 42 percent. If the net income had been *more* than predicted, some of the shares would have been rescinded. Your agreement should provide for the investor to *give up* shares if the company exceeds the original projections. It isn't equitable to give him the benefit of this protection without corresponding incentives to the company's founders. There are a number of possible variations on this equity adjustment agreement, and it's a good idea for your CPA and attorney to actively participate in its creation.

The agreement can be a most useful tool in persuading an otherwise hesitant investor to take the plunge. But you should probably reserve it only as a backup plan. If offered to one investor you should, in all fairness, make the same offer to all investors, even those who have already invested. Remember that if you treat your investors in a fair and equitable manner, they will support your business through good times and bad.

SHOULD YOU ISSUE STOCKS, BONDS, OR CONVERTIBLE SECURITIES?

The term "security" refers to a stock or bond. Many different instruments exist within these two general categories, and the creative people on Wall Street are inventing new hybrids almost every day. There are, however, several basic types of securities that are commonly used for capitalizing private companies.

Simplicity is important when creating the capital structure of a private company. You don't want investors to be confused by an overly complicated mix of strange-sounding types of stocks and bonds. You can always change the structure after the business has been established.

The following is a list of brief definitions of the more common securities:

• COMMON STOCK: This is the most acceptable type of security because all investors understand what it is. Each share of stock represents an equal portion of the ownership of the company, usually with one vote per share. This form of stock is usually recommended for a company's initial capitalization.

• PREFERRED STOCK: Usually issued to give the investor a little more peace of mind. Preferred stock provides the holder with a preferential claim to the assets of the corporation in the event that the corporation is liquidated. Preferred stockholders would receive all or a portion of their money back before the common stockholders are compensated. This type of stock also often carries preferred dividends, which guarantee that preferred stockholders' dividends will be paid before any dividends are paid to the common stockholders. Preferred stock usually does not have voting power.

• BONDS: A bond, also referred to as a "debenture," represents money loaned to a company. Payments of interest are made at regular intervals, usually every six months. The principal, or "face value," is repaid at some given point in the future. A bond is very similar to a promissory note, except that its terms are more standardized. Like a promissory note, the bond may be collateralized by a specific asset, it may be guaranteed by another party, or it may be unsecured.

The most important distinction between a bond and either common or preferred stock is that the bond is *not* "equity" in the company. It doesn't represent an ownership interest. However, a bond *may* be of a special type that is convertible *into* stock.

• CONVERTIBLE SECURITIES: A convertible security can either be preferred stock or a bond/debenture. This type of security has all the normal characteristics of a preferred stock or bond, but it also has an additional feature: It can be converted into common stock if the holder elects to do so. Each convertible bond or share of preferred stock can be exchanged for a fixed number of shares of common stock.

Which Is the Easiest Security to Sell to Investors?

Of the securities described, the *easiest* to sell is the convertible debenture. Why? Because you are essentially saying to the investor, "We'll pay back your money, with interest, if you are not satisfied with the progress of the company."

Naturally, the same things that make this deal advantageous to the investor make it less appealing to the entrepreneur. You are still in a better position by issuing simple common stock.

One other consideration of possible importance is that the IRS may not allow you to elect to be taxed as an S corporation if you have preferred stock or convertible debentures. We have discussed the importance of that tax treatment in Chapter Three, but you should discuss this potential tax problem with your attorney and accountant as well.

The best tool for raising money is common stock. Any other type of instrument should only be used as a last resort to convince a reluctant investor.

Final Thoughts: Persistence and Planning

By following the suggestions in this chapter, your chances for success in raising money will be increased significantly.

Everything you attempt will not meet with complete success the first time you try it. If you meet with failure, simply adjust your approach and keep trying. The investment capital you need *is* out there, and by applying the strategies and techniques discussed in this chapter and elsewhere in this book, you *will* be successful in finding the money you need.

CHAPTER 5

USING FINANCIAL STATEMENTS AND FORECASTS TO RAISE MONEY

Your ideas reflected in dollars and cents

In This Chapter:

1. Using financial statements in the business world
2. Financial statements in the business plan
   a. What bankers and lenders look for
   b. What potential investors look for
3. Format is as important as content
4. How to get started on projections
5. The forecasted projection
6. The *Use of Proceeds* Statement
7. Speaking the language of the money men

USING FINANCIAL STATEMENTS IN THE BUSINESS WORLD

For many people who are not already familiar with financial statements, the thought of having to use them in their business brings a certain degree of apprehension. After all, financial statements deal with issues that are often complex, seemingly arcane, and which have a language all their own.

Financial statements play an exceptionally important role

in business. Just as the goal of a business is to make a profit, so are financial statements the "scoreboard" that's used to monitor the success of the business in reaching that goal.

A Vital Component of Business Plans

Financial statements and projections also play an important part in a business plan or a request for financing. Investors and lenders want to see the businesses they invest in be profitable; and financial statements are the only way they have of tracking those profits. The information contained in the financial statements is their news report on their investment.

For all of these reasons, it is crucial that you know enough about financial statements to put them to use and to know how others will be using them. If you're willing to take an interest in them, the mystery of financial statements is suprisingly easy to penetrate.

Major Types of Statements

There are three major categories of financial statements in the business world: External Financial Reports, Internal Management Reports, and Projected Financial Statements.

External Financial Reports
These reports are what usually come to mind when someone refers to "financial statements." They give information about an *existing* company—one engaged in buying and selling, employing workers, making a product, or supplying some service. The company has produced revenues from its sales and has incurred operating expenses, resulting in a profit or a loss.

External financial reports, usually referred to simply as the "financial statements," (as if there were no other types) show the amounts of revenues and expenses the company has incurred, as well as the company's financial condition at the time the statements are produced. The statements are usually produced for the sake of outsiders, such as stockholders, potential investors, or lenders. Most of this chapter will deal with these "external" financial statements.

Internal Management Reports

These are similar to the external "financial statements" described above, except that they are often limited to a specific area of the company's financial performance, while covering that area in greater detail. These statements are usually produced for the benefit of the company's management, giving them the information they need to determine the efficiency or profitability of particular segments of the business. As such, these statements are rarely seen by outsiders.

An example of an internal management report would be a breakdown of sales by salesperson or by territory, showing how much of a company's sales were produced by each salesperson, or what percentage of the overall sales came from each geographic region the company serves. A report such as this would be used by the owner of the company, or by the sales managers, to judge how well each of the company's salespeople were performing, or which areas of the territory might need special attention.

Projected Financial Statements

Projected financial statements are also known by the terms "Pro-Forma Financial Statements" and, in the last few years, "Forecasted Financial Statements." This latter term has recently become the more accepted *formal* title for these statements, and most statements will now actually say "Forecasted Financial Statements" on the title page. But, from years of habit, most businesspeople, bankers, and investors will still refer to them as "Projections."

Projections deal with the future, and are basically "educated guesses" as to how a company will fare in the future. Obviously, if you are trying to start a *new* business and are putting together a business plan to help you develop and achieve your goals (one of which is to raise startup money), these projections will be your *only* statements. Your company will not have a financial history that could be reported in standard financial statements or in management reports.

On the other hand, if you were preparing to *expand* your existing business, then your business plan would include *both* standard financial statements (reflecting the company's past history) and projected financial statements (showing what you plan to accomplish in the future). For the moment, we will deal only with External Financial Reports, or "standard" financial statements, skipping Projected Financial Statements until the end of the chapter.

HOW FINANCIAL STATEMENTS ARE USED IN A BUSINESS PLAN

If you're putting financial statements into a business plan, the chances are that you're going to be approaching one (or both) of two groups with this information: bankers (or other lenders), or investors. Each of these groups has its own peculiarities when it comes to analyzing and interpreting financial statements.

What Bankers and Other Lenders Look For

The first thing to remember before you approach a banker is that he or she is unlikely to be a businessperson. Bankers have a well-earned reputation for being conservative. Although some individual bankers may be more willing than others to take a reasonable risk, they are generally much less likely than a venture capitalist or other potential investor to take a gamble on a business venture.

It's highly unlikely that you would be able to convince a banker to lend you startup capital for a new business with nothing more for collateral than the inventory or equipment you plan to buy with the bank's money. It might not be impossible, but it's not very probable, no matter how fantastically profitable your projected financial statements suggest that the business will be.

This is especially true if you have never managed a business like the one you are trying to start. In this case, there are innumerable unanswered questions in the banker's mind, all of which point to high risk as far as he or she is concerned. Unlike an investor, the banker can't expect a rate of return beyond that of a simple interest rate; as a result he is much less willing to take risks with the bank's money.

When you first approach a bank, you will probably work with a loan officer in the Commercial Loan Department. This officer will look over your financial statements and the rest of your business plan during your first visit, but probably won't go into the plan in too much detail. A meeting should be arranged for a later date, giving the banker time to review the business plan and the financial statements included in it.

Be Prepared to Explain Yourself
When it does come to the stage of review, though, remember that although most bankers don't have much real world business experience, they have certainly seen a *lot* of financial statements from businesses. This means you should be prepared to explain anything in the statements that they may not understand or that they might question.

This is a tremendous opportunity for you to show how well you know the financial intricacies of your business. To prepare for your meeting with the banker, we recommend a few sessions of questions and answers with your accountant. It will be time well spent, and will leave you well prepared for almost any question dealing with your company's financial statements.

Bankers' Loan Authorizations
Most individual bank loan officers have what is called "signature authority" for a specific amount, meaning they can loan any amount up to that ceiling without getting prior approval from the bank's loan committee. The amount of this signature authority is usually somewhere between $10,000 and $100,000, depending upon the size of the bank, the individual banker's experience, and his or her seniority.

Obviously, loans that do not exceed the officer's signature authority require less paperwork for the officer, and are generally easier to acquire. You might want to begin your banking relationship by requesting a loan which is within this limit.

Comparing Your Financial Statements to "Industry Standards"
When a loan request is to be presented to the loan committee of the bank, and often in *any* loan request, the loan officer will

need to know whether your financial statements and projections are reasonable. How does a banker, who has no practical experience in any business other than banking, decide what is "reasonable" for a dry-cleaning or equipment manufacturing company?

It's simple: They look in a book entitled *Annual Statement Studies*. This book contains five years of trend data on some 350 separate industries, and gives 17 commonly used financial ratios for each. You can probably find a copy of the book in the Reference Section of your local library; if not, it is available through the publisher, Robert Morris Associates.

The ratios your banker finds in this book are going to be *very* important to him, and it is very much to your advantage to know what he will be comparing you to. If your own financial statements or projections vary significantly from the ratios and percentages in the Statement Studies book, you should explain *why* they are different. *Don't let the banker realize you know about the book and are using it*—just take credit for being bright and knowledgeable about your industry.

Make sure your accountant gets a copy of the section of the book which deals with your industry, and ask him or her to explain what the ratios mean, and to compare your own financial statements to them. The ratios and percentages in the book will also help the accountant arrive at projections that are reasonable and realistic. Don't expect the accountant to know about this book before you tell him, though. Few people other than bankers are aware of it (unless they have read this book).

What Potential Investors Look For

As we discussed in our chapter on raising money, investors usually expect a fairly substantial return on their investment. This is reasonable, as they are taking a significant risk with their capital.

Because investors are less adverse to taking risk than bankers, they place greater importance on your financial *projections*. Whereas most bankers think "collateral first, projections second," investors tend to think just the opposite.

If you had to know your financial statements and projections fairly well for the purposes of seeking a loan, you had better know them *intimately* when approaching an investor. A "professional" investor, in particular, has seen hundreds or even thousands of business plans and projections during his or her career, and you better believe that your statements will be closely scrutinized.

Unlike the banker, an investor is probably not going to refer to any books (such as the *Annual Statement Studies* volume we mentioned earlier) to determine the reasonableness of your financial projections. Instead, they will compare your financial reports to their own established parameters. This criteria is going to be much less formal than the bankers', based more on past experience and gut feeling than on formulas.

Many professional or sophisticated investors have a support group of legal and financial advisers who will help judge the merits of a particular proposal. The investor's advisers may even use some of the same sources to *check* your projections and assumptions as you used to *prepare* them, so be sure you've done all the research we suggested in earlier chapters. This is where accurate research really counts.

FORMAT IS AS IMPORTANT AS CONTENT

We mentioned that a potential investor has seen perhaps thousands of business plans and projected financial statements in his or her career. And the banker, although maybe to a lesser degree than the investor, has seen his share, too.

A business plan is formatted in a specific manner to give the outsider a quick summary of the business, and to provide a comprehensive ready reference to each section. This ensures that he won't reject the proposal just because it would take too much time to search through and find the facts needed to determine his level of interest.

This is also the reason that the format of the financial statements and projections is so important: The statements must present their financial information to the investor in a manner which is familiar to him, so that he can easily analyze them with a minimum of time and effort.

A sure turn-off to the professional investor is an obvious lack of understanding on the entrepreneur's part of the accepted format for financial statements. There *are no new and unique formats* for financial statements that are acceptable to those who earn their living interpreting those financial statements and making judgments about the viability of the business they represent.

Don't doom your business idea to defeat before it's even had a chance: Use the proper format and terminology for your financial statements. Any other decision on your part is a sure sign of naivete, and that is the last impression you want to make with investors or lenders.

To illustrate our point, we were once involved with two businessmen who were trying to raise money to start a manufacturing company. These two fellows were exceptionally bright, and both had been very successful in the management of a company very similar to the one they now wanted to start. This combination of experience and past success is usually very attractive to investors, and it elicited interest from a number of investors.

Meetings were set up with several potential investors. The businessmen came to the meetings armed with a business plan and financial projections.

Both entrepreneurs were so intimately involved with the management aspects of their other business that they understood every detail of the finances involved, from the smallest element of cost overruns, to waste reports and inventory shrinkage. Because of this extensive experience, they had extremely detailed internal management reports (used in their past efforts), which they decided to use as the basis for their financial projections.

The reasoning was that this format would give potential investors every bit of detail they could possibly ask for. The problem was that these reports were so complex and specialized that it would have taken a business analyst who specialized in this particular type of manufacturing to read and interpret them. The businessmen were convinced that all this extra information would be an asset to them in trying to raise money, but they were in for a surprise: None of the investors they met were interested in pursuing the project.

The investors had all found the financial information too complex for them to be able to analyze in a reasonable length of time. They needed to be able to tell with a quick review if the business met their minimum standards, and if it warranted spending more time to study the details.

The investors were accustomed to seeing financial statements presented in certain standard formats, and when they saw formats which were foreign to them, they were simply unwilling to invest the time necessary to see if they made sense. Unable to do a quick review of the statements, they went on to other potential investments that were easier to analyze.

The two aspiring businessmen eventually enlisted the aid of a CPA who had experience with both financial projections and with manufacturing companies. The CPA translated their financial data into concise, standard financial statement form, and used the detailed initial work they had done as supporting footnotes. They reapproached some of the investors, and this time met with success.

The lesson to be learned here is that *format is nearly as important as content* in financial statements, especially if the statements are being used to raise capital or to obtain loans. Investors and loan officers have seen enough financial statements in their careers to quickly decipher and use them. But the statements must be presented in a manner that is familiar to them, or they will have to devote far too much time to their analysis. This is why you should never insert "do-it-yourself" financial statements in a serious business plan.

The "Standard" Financial Statements

Look at financial statements as if they were a language, one used to communicate the ideas of the financial world. Now imagine the chaos that would result if everyone invented their own unique dialect. No one could understand anyone else without spending extra time to learn the other person's peculiar language.

Obviously, the wheels of the business world would turn much more slowly if this were the case. Somewhere along the line, someone or some group of people had to standardize the financial language so that everyone understood everyone else. That group (in the United States) was the American Institute of Certified Public Accountants (AICPA).

AICPA developed what are known as Generally Accepted Accounting Principles, referred to most often by their initials, GAAP (pronounced gap, rhyming with lap). This is the common language—the rules used in the accounting world.

These rules guide and direct accountants as to what types of statements should be produced, what should go where on those statements, and in how much detail it should be shown. Nearly every possible contingency has been covered by the rules and guidelines of GAAP, and it is GAAP financial statements that both investors and financial institutions expect to see when they look at a business plan or other financial report.

GETTING STARTED ON PROJECTIONS

After having located the right accountant for your particular situation, what do you do next?

Begin with Basic Assumptions

If you're still in the startup phase—trying to put projected financial statements together for your business plan—you'll need to gather together a group of financial "assumptions." These assumptions are the basic foundation for your financial statements. What you are going to prepare are "projections" of the future, so called because you project a future outcome based upon a set of given assumptions.

These assumptions will include such questions as: How much of a particular item can I sell? At what price? How fast will sales grow? What will each item cost? How many employees will be needed? How much will they be paid?

Ask for Professional Assistance

Get started on your assumptions by asking your accountant to furnish copies of the financial statement of a similar business, or several similar types of businesses. (The photocopy should certainly have the name of the company removed from it, as well as any other identifying characteristics. If it doesn't, and your accountant has given you one of his other clients' financial statements without his consent, you should probably change accountants: The same thing may happen to you in the future.)

Begin your task by penciling in your projected revenues, or at least by guessing (assuming) the number of items you think you would be able to sell in your first month. Try to complete your projections for the first month of operations and then move on to the second month. How much will business increase in each of these successive months? What additional costs will you incur as sales increase?

Put Your Research to Work

During the course of your research, you will probably find industry averages for such items as costs of sales, average payroll costs, and average accounts receivables. Put these numbers to use, comparing them to what *you* think you will actually do.

Have your accountant review your initial figures and make suggestions. Factor in all the actual costs you can obtain, such as lease expenses and insurance costs. (Call your insurance agent if you need to get an estimate.) Calculate how many employees will be needed on each shift, as well as "administrative" employees like secretaries and bookkeeping staff, and decide how much it will cost to employ them.

Remember, these costs will increase as your business grows, so be sure to note which ones can be expected to increase.

Get Feedback from Others

When you have compiled as many of these numbers as possible, set up an appointment with your accountant to review your "assumptions." Ask him to compare your amounts against the percentages and ratios in the "Annual Statement Studies" book, and to explain what these ratios mean and how they relate to your company.

Your accountant will question some of your basic assumptions and your projected costs and sales. Try not to be defensive when you respond to this questioning; you could risk intimidating him into accepting what may be faulty assumptions. Encourage his input and ideas, and be willing to change some of your numbers if it seems reasonable to do so.

It's Difficult to Be Too Conservative

There is one consistent rule which we have found to be true when people begin estimating their future sales and expenses: They are nearly *always* too liberal with sales and too conservative with expenses.

It is impossible to tell until several years later, of course, but it seems as though there are always unexpected costs to be encountered, and that sales do not grow quite as quickly as expected. It is very rare to find a business that has met or exceeded its projections, and when one does, it is usually because those projections were produced using *ultra-conservatism*. This ultra-conservatism should be used by you when you begin your estimates for your projections. Nothing will scare away potential investors or lenders faster than seeing financial projections which they *know* are unattainable. These people would prefer to see a projection with room for error built into it, because they know what *you need to know*: More business ventures are destroyed by undercapitalization than by any other single factor.

Be Sure to Project Against Real Needs

If your investors and lenders review your projections and come to the conclusion that you don't even know how much money you really *need*, they certainly aren't going to be willing to finance you. So when you work on your financial statements, don't "cheat" yourself by trying to cut every cost to a minimum. Leave yourself enough slack in your estimates that you're *positive* you will be able to match them in the real world. If you're lucky, and conservative enough, you *may* actually meet your projections.

THE FORECASTED FINANCIAL PROJECTION

A more detailed analysis of financial statements appears in Appendix B, so we will omit most of those details here. But it would be helpful for you to have some idea of what your projections will look like when your accountant has compiled them for you. Table 5–1 shows a very simplified example of a

Forecasted Financial Statement (or "Projected Financial Statement," or "Pro-Forma Statement").

Notice that these projections are done on a monthly basis, with a summary of the year appearing in the last column. A projection similar to this one is usually done for each of the first two years the company will be in business, showing the month-to-month results of operations. The totals for each of these first two years are then shown on a second type of projection, on which totals for years three, four, and five will also appear (see Table 5–2).

Five Years Is a Long Time

One of your first reactions upon seeing this statement may be "Year *Five*? How am I supposed to know what will happen in five years?"

Just remember that these projections are only *estimates* of what you think will happen in the future. No one expects you to achieve exactly what you project, and the projections for the more distant years will certainly be less accurate than those for Year One.

But projecting your figures for five years does show the investor that you've given some thought to what may happen over the long term. And that's important, because you will need to have long-range goals to build your company strategy. Remember that the value of your company to the investor depends almost entirely upon its future earnings potential. Your five-year projections show what this potential might be.

THE *USE OF PROCEEDS* STATEMENT

Another peculiar feature of these projections is what happens in the first month of the first year: Sales are reflected as having begun in that *very first month*. If you're at all familiar with starting a project as complex as a business, you may wonder how you could accomplish all the tasks you need to do before actually opening your doors for business, and still have sales coming in for the first month.

The answer is simple: Month One of the projections is not

TABLE 5–1
Forecasted (Pro-Forma) Statement of Income: One Year of Operations

Sample Company, Incorporated
Forecasted Statement of Income
First Twelve Months of Operations

		Month One	Month Two	Month Three	Month Four	Month Five	Month Six	Month Seven
Sales Revenue	(1)	$75,000	$86,250	$99,188	$114,066	$131,175	$150,852	$173,480
Cost of Sales	(2)	$33,750	$38,812	$44,635	$51,330	$59,028	$67,884	$78,066
Gross Profit		$41,250	$47,438	$54,553	$62,736	$72,147	$82,968	$95,414
Less:								
Operating Expense	(3)	$11,550	$13,282	$15,275	$17,566	$20,201	$23,231	$26,716
Marketing Costs	(4)	$4,950	$5,693	$6,546	$7,528	$8,658	$9,956	$11,450
Depreciation	(5)	$11,500	$11,500	$11,500	$11,500	$11,500	$11,500	$11,500
Total		$28,000	$30,475	$33,321	$36,594	$40,359	$44,687	$49,666
Net Pre-Tax Income		$13,250	$16,963	$21,232	$26,142	$31,788	$38,281	$45,748
Tax Expense	(6)	$2,650	$3,393	$4,247	$5,228	$6,358	$7,656	$9,149
Net Monthly Income		$10,600	$13,570	$16,985	$20,914	$25,430	$30,625	$36,599
Prior Month's Income		$0	$10,600	$24,170	$41,155	$62,069	$87,499	$118,124
Year-to-Date Net Income		$10,600	$24,170	$41,155	$62,069	$87,499	$118,124	$154,723

TABLE 5-1—Continued

Sample Company, Incorporated
Forecasted Statement of Income
First Twelve Months of Operations

		Month Eight	Month Nine	Month Ten	Month Eleven	Month Twelve	First-Year Totals
Sales Revenue	(1)	$199,501	$229,427	$263,841	$303,417	$348,929	$2,175,126
Cost of Sales	(2)	$89,775	$103,242	$118,729	$136,538	$157,018	$978,807
Gross Profit		$109,726	$126,185	$145,112	$166,879	$191,911	$1,196,319
Less							
Operating Expense	(3)	$30,723	$35,332	$40,631	$46,726	$53,735	$334,968
Marketing Costs	(4)	$13,168	$15,142	$17,414	$20,025	$23,029	$143,559
Depreciation	(5)	$11,500	$11,500	$11,500	$11,500	$11,500	$138,000
Total		$55,391	$61,974	$69,545	$78,251	$88,264	$616,527
Net Pre-Tax Income		$54,335	$64,211	$75,567	$88,628	$103,647	$579,792
Tax Expense	(6)	$10,867	$12,842	$15,113	$17,726	$20,730	$115,959
Net Monthly Income		$43,468	$51,369	$60,454	$70,902	$82,917	$463,833
Prior Month's Income		$154,723	$198,191	$249,560	$310,014	$380,916	$0
Year-to-Date Net Income		$198,191	$249,560	$310,014	$380,916	$463,833	$463,833

TABLE 5–2

Forecasted (Pro-Forma) Statement of Income: Years One through Five

Sample Company, Incorporated
Forecasted Statement of Income
First Five Years of Operations

		Year One	Year Two	Year Three	Year Four	Year Five	Five-Year Totals
Sales Revenue	(1)	$2,175,126	$2,501,394	$2,876,603	$3,308,093	$3,804,307	$14,665,523
Cost of Sales	(2)	$978,807	$1,125,627	$1,294,471	$1,488,642	$1,711,938	$6,599,485
Gross Profit		$1,196,319	$1,375,767	$1,582,132	$1,819,451	$2,092,369	$8,066,038
Less:							
Operating Expense	(3)	$334,968	$385,215	$442,997	$509,446	$585,864	$2,258,490
Marketing Costs	(4)	$143,559	$165,092	$189,856	$218,334	$251,084	$967,925
Depreciation	(5)	$138,000	$155,000	$159,000	$190,000	$211,000	$853,000
Total		$616,527	$705,307	$791,853	$917,780	$1,047,948	$4,079,415
Net Pre-Tax Income		$579,792	$670,460	$790,279	$901,671	$1,044,421	$3,986,623
Tax Expense	(6)	$115,959	$134,092	$158,056	$180,334	$208,884	$797,325
Net Annual Income		$463,833	$536,368	$632,223	$721,337	$835,537	$3,189,298
Prior Year's Income		$0	$463,833	$1,000,201	$1,632,424	$2,353,761	$0
Cumulative Five-Year Total Net Income		$463,833	$1,000,201	$1,632,424	$2,353,761	$3,189,298	$3,189,298

necessarily the first month you start *preparing* to do business. Instead, it is the first month you actively begin selling to the public—or trying to do so. It is the first month your normal monthly operations are underway.

What about all the time between now and that first month you begin selling? There are a lot of things that must be done, and most of them take money to accomplish. You might need to sign a lease and begin paying monthly rent while installing equipment. You might need to purchase this equipment several months prior to actively starting the business. You might need to start training employees.

Where are these costs accounted for so that a potential investor can see where a big portion of his startup money is going? These expenditures are shown in a brief, but very important statement titled "Use of Proceeds."

The Use of Proceeds statement gives an estimate of what you will do with the money you raise during the startup phase of your business. It tells investors how their money will be spent. If you go to the bank for a personal loan—for example, a home improvement loan or an auto loan—the bank usually wants to know to what use you are putting the money. They want to be sure that the money is being properly used, just as your investors do. The Use of Proceeds statement gives them this information. (The example below should occupy one full page. Accompanying Notes would follow on the next page(s).)

Use of Proceeds

Acquisition of plant & equipment (1)	$900,000
Marketing costs (2)	100,000
Reimbursement of expenses (3)	20,000
Working capital (4)	250,000
	$1,270,00

(See accompanying notes)

A Brief Statement

Notice how little detail appears on the face of this statement. Its purpose is not to tell where every single penny will be spent, but only to give potential investors the ability, at a glance, to tell where the startup capital is going.

The categories of expenditures are all broad; "Plant & equipment," for instance, would include everything from a building the company might purchase to copy machines for the offices. Wherever the reader might want additional information, they can refer to the "accompanying notes," identified by the numbers in parentheses, (1), (2), etc.

To develop this example of the Use of Proceeds Statement, the following might be the notes of explanation for the various amounts shown on the face of the statement.

Notes to Use of Proceeds Statement

1. Acquisition of plant & equipment—Management has signed a contract to purchase a manufacturing facility located at 31080 W. Bayshore Drive, Bluntsville, NY. A downpayment of $300,000 (30 percent of the purchase price of $1,000,000) will be made at closing, with the balance of approximately $700,000 financed by the seller on a land contract at 11 percent interest over a period of ten years. Manufacturing equipment and tooling will require a cash investment of approximately $500,000. Office equipment amounting to an estimated $100,000 will be purchased out of proceeds and will be installed in the plant facility.

2. Marketing costs—The Company has arranged for the creation of a four-color, ten-page brochure to be used to establish initial accounts for the Company's products. The cost of 50,000 brochures will be approximately $45,000, including artwork, color separations, typesetting, and printing. Mailing costs, including postage and rental of mailing lists, will be $15,000. The remaining $40,000 allocated for marketing costs is budgeted for print advertising in trade magazines, creative expenses, and for the production of Company stationery, business forms, and exterior signs.

3. Reimbursement of expenses—Certain officers and stockholders of the Company have advanced legal and accounting fees in the amount of $20,000. These fees were incurred in relation to the promulgation of this offering.

4. Working capital—To be used for normal operating expenses and as a reserve against contingencies.

The Notes Give Necessary Detail

These "Notes" are an important part of the statement, because they provide information on the planned use of the funds, while allowing the Use of Proceeds statement itself to remain simple and easy to read. Lenders and investors want to be sure that funds are going to be used wisely, and would surely question your business judgment if the notes disclosed that the $900,000 the Company plans to spend on "plant and equipment" were going to include $800,000 for a business jet.

SPEAK THE LANGUAGE OF THE BUSINESS WORLD

Whether you have a business with an actual operating history, or you have a new startup, the financial statements will give the prospective investor or lender the information they need to judge the economic viability of your proposal. As part of your business plan, these financial statements will have at least as much impact on your chances of obtaining funding as will any other component of your plan.

Be thorough, objective, conservative, and realistic when compiling your financial statements. Use an experienced professional accountant to assist you in their preparation.

Follow these rules, and you will immeasurably increase your chances of finding the money you need. If, instead, you use a format of your own creation, and include blindly optimistic assumptions, you will find it nearly impossible to obtain any money from investors or lenders.

Speak the language of the money men, and they will listen to you. Speak instead a language of your own invention and no one will understand you—or even listen.

CHAPTER 6

HOW TO ACQUIRE AND
FINANCE A BUSINESS

---

*It's easier, cheaper, faster ... to acquire an existing
company than to start one from scratch.*
Drucker

In This Chapter:

1. Acquiring an existing business: advantages and disadvantages
2. A key question: Why are they selling?
3. The acquisition search
4. Qualifying the candidates
5. Evaluating the companies
6. Negotiations: strategy and tactics
7. Making the offer
8. Closing the deal

ACQUIRING AN EXISTING BUSINESS:
ADVANTAGES AND DISADVANTAGES

The prospect of starting a business can be overwhelming. It
might seem preferable to step right into the profits and rewards
of an existing, successful business.

There *are* advantages in acquiring a company that has
already put its growing pains behind it. Yet there are also dan-

gers and pitfalls that should be avoided. These risks, present in every acquisition, can be minimized by applying the techniques and tactics described in this chapter.

A diligent acquisition requires hard work. Many hours must be spent on each step of the acquisition process—the search, the negotiation, the financing, the closing, and the transition.

Buying a business is by no means an overnight process. It can take from four to ten months, or longer, to complete. During this period any number of things could kill the deal; and about half of the acquisitions that reach the negotiation stage fall through. For this reason, at least two acquisition candidates—the more the better—should be pursued simultaneously, depending on the time that can be devoted to the project.

Advantages of Buying an Existing Business

Time

The first advantage in buying an existing business is one of *time*. Instead of going through a time-consuming startup period, a buyer can step right into a going concern.

Now don't misunderstand what this means. The acquisition process itself takes about the same amount of time as starting a *new* business. It isn't startup time that is saved. What is saved is the time normally required to *build* a company after getting it started.

An acquired business will have already gone through its tough growth stage. It has already found and trained employees, established relationships with suppliers, and built a solid customer base. It will have already experienced its growing pains and, hopefully, will have ironed them out.

Naturally, any business will have to have been in operation for a reasonable period of time to be sure it's really past those growing pains. Five or more years of operating history will show how a business weathers changes in the economic climate. It's imperative to see results from both good and bad times, as some companies have good profits for a few years, and then are nearly wiped out by an economic swing.

Track Record

One of the most significant advantages of an existing business is that it will possess an actual operating history. This is a real record of how the company has fared, not just how the management *hoped* it would fare. This operating history is infinitely more reliable than the tenuous projections of a startup.

The company's financial history can be used to realistically project future performance. It can also be used to establish a value for the company relative to other firms in the same industry. This proven performance also makes the business more attractive to the many investors and lenders who aren't pure speculators.

Customers

Perhaps the biggest advantage an existing business offers over a startup is an irreplaceable asset—the customer. A business cannot make money until customers are convinced to buy and keep buying. In the jargon of the business and financial world, the value of the buying public's awareness and acceptance of a company's products, services, and image is called *goodwill*. Goodwill is considered an asset, just like inventory or real estate.

Ideally, a business is identified with a positive image: Products are of a good quality and fairly priced, and personnel are friendly and helpful. If a new company were to try to build this kind of positive reputation among consumers, it would take a *minimum* of a year. A successful, established business already has it.

Disadvantages of Buying an Existing Business

Premium Price

Little of value in life is free. And this is the principal disadvantage of buying an established company: A solid and profitable business will command a premium price.

Any company that is earning consistent, healthy profits will cost substantially more than would be required to start a similar business. If it doesn't, then something is wrong— look closely! Of course, the cost of leading a startup company through its adolescence is much higher than the simple startup costs. All that experience is "paid for" through the painful process of trial and error.

No Guarantees

There can be other disadvantages to acquiring an established business. There is no guarantee that the established methods, personnel, and image of an existing company are necessarily the best that are possible.

Some companies operate for years, and operate profitably, even while doing some basic things incorrectly. This gradually erodes the public's confidence and trust. A business such as this is a time bomb waiting to explode. And it may go off in the acquirer's face.

It is essential that a problem business be identified *prior* to its acquisition. The techniques described in this chapter will help with this identification.

WHY ARE THEY SELLING?

This is the first and most important question to be asked when considering the purchase of an existing business. The *real* answer can speak volumes about the business.

It can't be emphasized enough how important it is to keep this question in mind during all the stages of the negotiations. Pay attention to *all the signs* that emanate from the seller, the employees, and the business itself.

There are plenty of good and legitimate reasons for someone to sell his business. The owner may simply be tired of the daily demands of running a business—after all, it isn't easy. He may have built the business and now wants to cash out. The sale of his company may be the only way he can enjoy the fruits of his labor. (A business, much like a piece of real estate that has appreciated in value, must be *sold* before its full value can be realized in cash.)

Perhaps the owner is reaching retirement age and has no children who are interested in the business. Or the seller may want to devote time to some other project. Maybe he yearns for the challenge of creating a new business. Even "burn-out" can be a legitimate reason to sell. John Madden successfully coached the Oakland Raiders to a Super Bowl championship and then resigned, citing burn-out as his reason for quitting coaching. Mid-life crisis is real, and it happens all the time.

Whatever their reason for selling, it's imperative that you be certain you have discovered it.

Sellers are probably going to stretch the truth a bit in describing the value and potential of their business. Expect some exaggeration—some "puffery"—from them. Don't be offended by it. But be alert to a business being sold for the wrong reason. Its owner may be very unscrupulous, and may misrepresent or actually lie about past profits and future potential.

One of the authors represented an acquirer who was interested in entering the Florida home furnishings market. A search turned up several candidates, one of which was a company in the carpet business.

During the examination stage of the acquisition process, the author visited the facilities, met with management, and went over the financial statements of the prospective seller. Everything seemed in order, and the client authorized the author, in his role as acquisition consultant, to move into the analysis stage.

After some careful checking and verification, the consultant found that the seller had created an entire set of misleading financial statements for the sole purpose of attracting a buyer. The carpet company was actually in financial trouble.

This company—apparently established—had shown, by financial statements set up on its own in-house computer, annual sales in excess of $12 million and after tax profit of more than $1.5 million; in reality, it had sales of $8 million and an operating loss.

Obviously, discussions were immediately broken off with the sellers. The owners had apparently realized that their company was losing its competitive edge, and had decided to sell it any way that they could. Their sucker never came along, however, and creditors eventually forced the company to liquidate.

Pay close attention to details; use professional assistance

(especially a good accountant); be wary, and follow proven step-by-step procedures. These precautions will help you to avoid the scams and losers.

THE ACQUISITION SEARCH

The best acquisition candidates are seldom found by looking in the Business Opportunities section of the local newspaper. The best candidates come from a well-organized search.

Step One: Establish Objectives

This first step, surprisingly, is frequently neglected. Without a focus, many hours and countless dollars could be wasted. Be astute in this regard, and establish objectives and parameters *before* launching the search.

Begin by deciding on two basic objectives: 1) The industry or industries you would like to be in, and 2) The specific businesses within that industry that you would prefer. Remember that the more that is known about a particular field and the greater your experience in that industry, the better your chance of success. Stick with the familiar. No one wants an expensive lesson in the intricacies of an unfamiliar business. Choose the industry carefully. Then select several businesses within that industry that are best suited to your knowledge, experience, and talents.

Step Two: Select a Geographic Area

There may be some very compelling reasons to stay put. But the acquisition of a business can open up new vistas for the buyer. You should at least *consider* relocating if it helps improve the chances of success. No rules prevent an acquirer from considering several geographic areas.

Be sure to talk this over with family and any partners. Do some research on which areas of the country are best for the type of business that's been selected. Then make a decision on the region best suited to you and your selected business.

Step Three: Establish Criteria

Establish a set of criteria by which to judge the prospective businesses. These criteria will be arbitrary values determined by your unique abilities and limitations—things such as financial status and the ability to manage people. There is some soul-searching and financial figuring that must be done before complete and useful criteria can be created. And you should read this entire book before establishing the criteria called for here.

One criterion you will need to consider is the range of size for the business you seek. This limit will be affected mostly by your ability to finance the purchase. "Size" refers to value of the business—selling price—as well as number of employees, annual revenues, profitability, and net worth.

Another important criterion is the *age* of the business. It is recommended that only businesses at least five years old be considered. Statistics indicate that most businesses don't make it to the fifth year. The fact that a business has endured that long is a point in its favor. According to a Dun & Bradstreet report in 1985, 56.3 percent of the businesses that were between one and five years old at the time, failed during that year.

Another reason for considering only companies with five or more years of experience is that they will most probably have gone through one complete economic cycle. Participating in a complete economic cycle means that a business and its management have likely matured. The performance over that complete economic cycle is a measure of both the strength of the business and the industry it is in.

Step Four: Locating Acquisition Candidates

If care isn't taken at this stage of the search, then the whole affair is most likely to be nothing more than a waste of time and money. Companies must be found that are genuinely for sale (this is sometimes more difficult to determine than it sounds). The companies that are located must also fit the criteria that the acquirer has established in Step Three.

Accurate Financial Statements

It is essential that an accurate financial history be obtained from the seller. Current financial condition is also important. Without these financial statements a buyer cannot get an accurate picture of the performance of the company.

When dealing with private companies there can be a major problem in getting accurate financial statements. An audit can be performed, of course, but this is both expensive and time-consuming. If the audit uncovers hidden problems, the acquirer is out the cost, which will probably range from $15,000 to $50,000 and more. The audit will have neutralized the danger of buying a business whose earnings or net worth had been misrepresented; but it won't bring another acquisition to the table. The acquirer may even find it necessary to start all over again.

There are some intelligent methods that can be used to reduce this risk, though. One of the best is to use CPA firms in the search process.

"Big Eight" CPAs: The Best Source

Begin the search for acquisition candidates with CPA firms. Their clients will have financial statements prepared in accordance with generally accepted accounting principles. In some cases, the statements will already have been reviewed or audited. In addition, the accountants who prepare the company's statements may offer some insight into the business itself. After all, they have a vested interest: they want to retain the business as a client after it's been sold.

Start with what are termed the "Big Eight" accounting firms (see Appendix A). They're likely to have the largest roster of clients.

The following sample letter can be used to approach these CPA firms about prospective acquisition companies:

> Dear ____:
>
> I/We are interested in acquiring an existing company and thought that you or one of your associates might have a client company that meets my/our requirements. We are somewhat flexible, but the ideal acquisition would be in the [consumer elec-

tronics] industry, preferably a [wholesale distributor], located in [the southeastern portion of Florida]. To be considered, the company must be at least five years old and profitable, with revenues of [$5 million to $15 million], and a positive net worth. Current management should be willing to remain with the company, although the length of that employment is negotiable. I will be phoning you to discuss this in more detail.

Very truly yours,

The criteria in the letter can be a bit more general than those established as guidelines for your search. This leaves the door open for a company that is similar enough to be acceptable. Once several candidates have been found, more specific criteria can be applied to help decide which of them to pursue most aggressively.

Establish a Relationship
Notice that the last line of the suggested letter states that you "will be phoning. . . to discuss this in more detail." The reason for that phone call is to establish a more personal relationship between the sender and the CPA. The phone call should lead to a meeting, and the meeting will lead to the CPA taking enough of a personal interest in the search to ensure that any qualified candidates will be remembered and referred.

Send personalized letters. Find the name of the "partner in charge" of each CPA office. To secure that partner's name simply call the firm and ask for it.

Other Professionals to Contact

Large Regional and Local CPA Firms. Don't ignore the larger CPA firms in the search for acquisition candidates, even though they may not be members of the Big Eight. Ask an attorney or banker for the names of the bigger of the local and regional firms.

Corporate or Securities Law Specialists. The third choice for obtaining acquisition candidates are attorneys who specialize in corporation law or securities law. Avoid writing to

attorneys who are in general practice, as well as those specializing in other areas of law. Attorneys can be located according
to their specialty in the Martindale-Hubbell Law Directory,
a reference book found in most libraries. Send them a letter
similar to the one used for CPAs.

In general, when dealing with attorneys, it's a good idea
to make sure that they are not charging for their time. Their
legal advice is not being sought. Fees for their time should
rightfully be the responsibility of their clients. It pays to clarify
this sometimes sticky point with them when you first make
contact.

Business Owners. The fourth target group for acquisition leads consists of individual businesses. Each successive
group or target is less likely to be fruitful than the one previous,
and diminishing results for time and effort will correspond with
every group beyond the CPAs.

Businesses which may fall within your established parameters can be located in directories published by Standard &
Poor's and Dun & Bradstreet. Companies are arranged in these
reference works by both geographic location and S.I.C. (Standard Industrial Classification). The listed information includes
their corporate name, address and phone number, approximate
annual revenues, and the names of officers and directors.

If you decide to target some of these businesses, you should
write directly to the Chairman of the Board or, if no Chairman
is listed, to the President. This letter will be completely different from the one sent to accountants and attorneys:

Dear Mr./Ms. ___:

I am presently conducting an acquisition search for a company
very much like [name of company].

You may not have ever considered selling your company, but,
if you might be interested, I would appreciate the opportunity to
discuss this possibility with you.

I am writing you as a principal, acting for myself and not
as an agent for anyone else. Your name and the name of your
company was obtained from [give the reference, such as Standard
& Poor's].

Please contact me at the above address or phone number if you wish to discuss this. Of course, there would be no obligation for either of us, and anything discussed would remain confidential.

Sincerely,

This letter is intended to be very direct and to answer the questions "Is this letter from some business broker or other intermediary?" and "How did they get my name?"

The recipients of the letter must make the next move. If they are interested in talking, they must call or write. Unlike the letters to CPAs and attorneys, *the sender does not call*. Why? Because a response by the business owner "qualifies" them. Time will be wasted talking to owners who show no interest in selling.

Unfortunately, even of these "self-qualifiers," a good percentage will be interested only in finding out what their business is worth to a prospective buyer. They will be after a free appraisal of sorts. So approach these prospects with care (see the next section, "Qualifying the Candidates").

Professional Intermediaries. There are some merger and acquisition intermediaries whose reputations are excellent. Many specialize in a particular industry or geographic area. They tend to deal with "middle market" companies—those with sales in the $1 million to $50 million range.

These professional intermediaries are, for the most part, not readily recognizable names. *The Wall Street Journal* sometimes carries advertisements for reputable intermediaries, and also prints notices of deals recently completed ("tombstones"). Scan the *Journal* for these companies, or do some digging in the library for directories of intermediaries.

Regional commercial banks have entered the intermediary business, as have some mid-size investment bankers. Two reputable firms whose names are heard somewhat frequently are The Geneva Companies and W. T. Grimm & Co. Geneva, headquartered in Costa Mesa, California, represents only sellers, and claims to be the largest dealmaker in this middle market segment. Grimm, out of Chicago, represents either buyer or seller, and is a subsidiary of Merrill Lynch Business Financial Services, Inc.

The biggest negative to dealing with companies such as Geneva or Grimm is that they negotiate with several buyers for a company at the same time. This could develop into a bidding war and cost the buyer more than might otherwise be necessary to acquire the business. It's an advantage for the seller, and clearly not for the buyer.

Business Opportunities Ads. The next choice for finding potential buyouts is *The Wall Street Journal's* Business Opportunity ads. They appear every weekday, although Business Opportunities are most prevalent on Tuesday, Wednesday, and Thursday. Most will include a brief description of the company being offered, and a box number for replies.

The Wall Street Journal makes a cursory effort to screen advertisers, but it is nearly impossible to tell if the ads are misleading. Many ads are placed by sales agents, intermediaries, and business broker types in an attempt to find clients. The businesses advertised may not even exist at the time you respond.

In truth, our experience with *Wall Street Journal* ads has not been good. When a genuine company was being offered at a reasonable price, we became one of many bidders. This is not the best situation to find yourself in as a buyer. For this same reason, the *Journal* is highly recommended to sellers, but buyers can do better by the methods covered earlier.

Miscellaneous Publications. There are a number of publications and listings distributed nationally which purport to list available businesses. It appears that these publications are little more than market-places for agents and brokers. There are few principals interested in buying or selling directly.

If a copy of these publications can be obtained without paying high subscription fees, it might be worthwhile to look at the companies they have listed. But be careful.

Business Brokers/Real Estate Agents. Even further down the list of potential acquisition sources are business brokers and real estate agents. These are the most aggressive of the intermediaries. Some are franchisees or licensees of national firms. Others are real estate agents representing the seller of a business—usually a small one.

Some business brokers and real estate agents are very knowledgeable, reputable, and professional. Many others know little about financial statements, and even less about the accuracy of the financial claims of their clients. Overall, it is probably best to avoid brokers and agents, unless their client looks especially attractive, owns a minimum five-year operating history, and has reliable financial statements.

QUALIFYING THE CANDIDATES

There are certain items and signals to look for when investigating acquisition candidates. A buyer should enter the qualifying process using the motto of the state of Missouri: "Show me." Several "musts" are outlined below, but nothing takes the place of good old common sense. If it doesn't feel right, don't proceed with it. Don't discount those sixth sense feelings; many times they're an accurate warning system.

Examine the Financial Statements

The first step in qualifying a company is to examine its financial statements. Some companies are reluctant to disclose their financial history and current condition to a prospective buyer. A serious buyer *must* be willing to sign a nondisclosure agreement. In fact, if a potential seller is hesitant in parting with financial statements, the buyer should *suggest* that a nondisclosure form be prepared. That usually convinces them that they are dealing with a bona fide buyer.

If the seller still refuses to provide financial statements, politely but firmly refuse to proceed any further. If information is hard to get at this early stage, it will continue to be hard to obtain later.

What Format Are the Statements in?

Once in possession of the financial statements (and notice how readily available they are from companies found through CPA firms), look at the format of the statements. Are they in standard form? Or are they obviously a do-it-yourself format?

Who Prepared the Statements?

Those prepared by a CPA or accounting firm will have the name of the preparer clearly printed on the statements or on the binder cover. A CPA statement will also include a cover letter stating the type of preparation work that was done: an *audit*, a *review*, or a *compilation*.

Ideally, a buyer would like *audited* statements. This means that the CPA firm has tested the figures for accuracy and validity. The next best is *reviewed*, meaning *some* (usually the most significant) of the figures have been tested for accuracy. But even a compilation prepared by a CPA is better than having the numbers thrown together by the sellers or their bookkeeper.

Some companies employ their own bookkeepers, and statements are often created by the bookkeeper using a drawer full of receipts, check stubs, and pay records. The information in these statements is often subject to the owner's "approval," and the accuracy of this type of financial statement is questionable at best.

Tax Returns

The tax returns of a company may be used as a limited alternative to financial statements, but they're really not as good.

There is an assumption in the business world—and it's usually a valid one—that revenues on a business's tax return will be reported at the lowest levels possible and that expenses will be shown as high as possible. This means the company would pay the lowest amount of tax. This should also mean that a company's prior five years' income tax returns would provide a very condensed, but reasonably conservative, set of financial statements.

One of the problems with this approach is that an unscrupulous seller might "doctor" the returns before providing them. This can be prevented by having an accountant prepare an IRS form entitled "Request for Copy of a Tax Return" for each of the years desired. The seller must sign the request so that the IRS will honor it, and the mailing address listed on the form should be that of the buyer or the buyer's accountant. The cost of this process is minimal, but it takes from eight to ten weeks to receive the copies.

Also, sellers have been known to overstate their income for tax purposes for one year, anticipating the sale of the business. To avoid this, be sure to request copies of several years' returns.

Be aware that these tax returns only show how the company has performed in the *past*—they don't present any information on the company's current financial position. A full-scale audit has to be undertaken for that. Lacking that, a CPA could provide a limited verification of certain items on the Balance Sheet. This is significantly less expensive than a full-scale audit.

Measure Against Criteria

After examining the financial statements for accuracy and format, compare them with the financial criteria established early in the acquisition search. Measure each acquisition candidate against acceptable ranges for sales, profitability, net worth, assets, and number of employees. Decide at this point whether to proceed further with a candidate. If the answer is "yes," then a few more qualifying steps are in order.

Speak Directly to the Seller

At this stage in the qualifying process, a buyer may not have met the seller personally. Talking to the seller prior to this point could be a waste of time.

No more than about 20 percent of the original candidates make it to this stage. Why talk to a seller if there's no actual interest in his company? Now that there *is* an interest, it is time to speak to the seller directly.

As the financial statements have been examined, and discussions held with accountants, questions have no doubt occurred to the buyer. Write these questions down as they come up. Refine the list prior to speaking with the owner.

A Visit to the Company

Call the owner and discuss what you can over the phone. If the answers and comments are encouraging, end the conversation by arranging for a personal visit to the place of business. This visit should be made during normal working hours. A potential buyer will want to see and *feel* the business while it is actually operating.

If the seller balks at this suggestion, offer to go along with any "cover" they might want to devise (a banker or a potential investor or some other person who wouldn't cause alarm among employees). Assure the seller of complete discretion. If the seller is reluctant, be firm. It is imperative to visit the business while it is actually operating.

"Feel" the business. On the visit, try to gain a general impression of the way it runs. The less said during this visit the better. Pay close attention to small things such as the cleanliness and neatness of the premises. Are the employees working at a normal pace? Do they seem tense? Are they happy? Is the building in disrepair? Are the bathrooms clean or dirty? Is the space cramped, well-utilized, or virtually empty? Are the storerooms well-stocked? Is the equipment in good condition; are the office machines new or beat up? Where do the employees park? Is the neighborhood safe? Pay attention to *everything*.

These initial visits are eye-opening experiences. If a picture is worth a thousand words, then a visit is worth a million.

Once the facilities have been toured, it is time to leave. Make it known in advance that a prior commitment limits the time available for this first visit. Head for some place where there are few distractions, and make some notes about the visit.

Record impressions in writing and as soon as possible. The

more time that passes, the less vivid the impressions. After finishing the notes, give the company a grade, ranking it on a scale of 1 to 10. Let this ranking be based solely on gut feeling at the time.

Look at the Competition

Take a little time before deciding whether there is a real interest in this acquisition candidate. If the feelings are negative, go on to another candidate. If the decision is to continue pursuing this company, there will be two things that must be done: (1) find out about the company itself, and (2) find out who its competition is.

Visit these competitors for a visual comparison. The latter is easy to accomplish if the company is in a retail business. If they are engaged in high-tech manufacturing, this personal visit may be difficult to manage. At the very least, drive by the competition's facilities. Look for that "feeling."

Of course, nothing prevents anyone from parking the car, walking to a business building, and asking to speak to the owner. If this direct approach is taken, however, it is a cardinal sin to divulge the name of the company you are considering acquiring.

EVALUATING THE COMPANIES

The acquisition search is, by this point, down to the best of the lot—those companies who have survived the preliminary inspection. Now an acquirer should begin looking at candidate companies under a microscope. How good is the business? What is it really worth? How much of the purchase price would have to be cash? How much can be borrowed against the business? How will the purchase be structured?

Proceeding step by step through all the points covered in this chapter, an acquirer will be able to make two intelligent decisions:

1. Whether or not to buy the company.
2. *How* to buy the company.

Comparative Analysis

Under careful analysis, financial statements reveal much more than just profit and loss. This analysis is so important that, after you've completed the steps outlined below, an experienced CPA should be retained to explain the statements and their comparisons to those of similar-type companies.

Appendix B contains a number of the ratios and percentages that allow a direct comparison of different businesses. Set up a table like Table 6–1, and fill in the information from the financial statements of the companies. Try to do the last five calculations in Table 6–1, without the help of an accountant, using the formulas in Appendix B. This will provide a better understanding of what these ratios and percentages really mean.

The answers to these questions indicate which one of the

TABLE 6–1
Analysis Worksheet

	Company 1	Company 2	Company 3
From the financial statements:			
Current assets			
"Quick" assets			
Current liabilities			
Total assets			
Total liabilities			
Total equity			
Sales			
Cost of sales			
Net income			
Calculations from above:			
Current ratio			
Quick ratio			
Sales to assets			
Cost of sales %			
Net income as % of sales			

companies has been best managed: Which is generating the highest net income? Which is generating sales most efficiently in terms of the use of its assets? Which one is the most "liquid"?

None of the numbers or ratios alone can determine if a business should be acquired. *No* business is a good buy, no matter how good its ratios, if it's priced too high. But if two different businesses having nearly identical assets, liabilities, and sales were for sale at the same price, then the one producing a higher net income on sales would obviously be the better buy. The ratios and percentages compare the *efficiency* of each company. This comparison is one more step toward identifying the best acquisition candidates.

Examine Owners' Salaries

Some owners pay themselves more than others, and it will be necessary to equalize salaries on the financial statements to keep comparisons fair.

As an example, Company A might show net income of $150,000 on its financial statements, whereas Company B shows $200,000. On the face of it, Company B appears to be more profitable. But the owner of Company B may pay himself only $25,000 per year. Company A's owner, on the other hand, may pull down a salary of $100,000 per year.

These salaries are treated as an expense to the company, but they're not necessarily what a buyer might take as a salary. So, to equalize the companies' net incomes, simply *add back* the owners' salaries.

	Company A	Company B
Net income per financial statements	$150,000	$200,000
Owner salaries	$100,000	$ 25,000
Adjusted net income	$250,000	$225,000

As you can see, Company A now looks like the better buy.

Research the Industry

Once you've finished with the financial statements, or perhaps while the CPA is looking at them, it is time to research the industry that the potential acquisition is in. The place to do this research is in the reference section of a public library.

See what the experts are saying. The best reference works are Standard & Poor's Industry Reports and various Department of Commerce Economic Reports and Forecasts. Then head for the library's Periodical Room to read some of the trade magazines for the industry. Ask librarians for help in locating this material, and ask them to suggest other helpful reference sources.

Research reports on specific industries can usually be found at major stock brokerage firms. These reports are prepared for investors and are usually available free of charge.

Look for Industry Trends. The overall trend in the industry of the target company is an important indicator of where that business may be headed in the near future. Is the industry in a downtrend, in an uptrend, or rolling along at a fairly predictable pace?

If the industry is in a downtrend, it may not be wise to enter it at all—you don't want to be selling buggy whips after automobiles have begun to crowd the roads.

If there is an uptrend, or if one is expected soon, a buyer may be acquiring a business that will grow automatically over the next several years. This growth, propelled by external forces and kept moving by sheer momentum, will provide a bonus: a margin for error. Inexperience and initial mistakes will be partially offset by the industry's uptrend.

On the other hand, an industry that is steady and predictable may offer less chance for growth, but will provide a steady stream of profit and cash flow. This will allow a buyer to plan and budget with a high level of confidence. This will make banks and lenders happy.

A steady no-growth industry shouldn't be shortchanged simply because it's less glamorous. Stability is a strong plus for the businessperson. Some entrepreneurs establish a base by acquiring a predictable, stable business, and then go on to start or acquire companies in riskier industries. This strategy offers both stability and the chance for rapid growth, and, very importantly, can limit the entrepreneur's downside risk.

Companies Mentioned in Reports. Some research reports mention companies by name. Take notes and begin to build a file on the companies that are of most interest. Especially note those that seem to be most representative of the market niche you wish to enter.

Publicly Held Companies Should Be Noted. Research and intelligence gathering can be done by finding these companies in Standard & Poor's Stock Reports. These are one-page summaries of recent business developments and financial statements.

The objective in researching public companies is twofold: First, you can find out how these companies are doing: Does their performance agree with what has been learned from the industry research you've done? If so, can you isolate some of the things they are doing right? Second, you can easily determine the value that the market has placed on these companies. One way to do this is to look at the current P/E (price to earnings) ratio of the company's stock. Another way is to compare multiples of sales or book value (net income relative to annual sales, or to net worth).

The P/E Ratio

The price to earnings ratio is a simple enough concept. It works like this: If a company's stock is selling at a price that is 10 times greater than its per share earnings, then its P/E ratio is 10. That means the total *value* of that company—as determined by an efficient free market—is 10 times the company's *total* annual net income. If the company is earning $200,000 annually, and its P/E ratio has been calculated at 10, then its *total* value is $2,000,000. And where do you find a specific P/E ratio? It's published in *The Wall Street Journal* every weekday, or in most other periodical stock listings.

The Problem with Valuations Using P/E.   Using a P/E ratio would make a valuation of a proposed acquisition seem easy. Simply find the average P/E ratio for those publicly traded companies most like the acquisition target. Then, multiply the average P/E by the current net income of the target company.

As an example, if the average P/E is 12, and the acquisition target is earning $100,000 per year, its value is theoretically $1,200,000 (12 times $100,000).

The problem with this is that we're comparing the P/E ratio of a publicly held company with that of a *private* one, and they're not the same animal at all.

The stock of a publicly held company is very liquid. If an investor decides to sell her stock, she can easily do so, probably on the same day she makes the decision to sell. A simple call to her stock broker is all it takes. But a private company doesn't give you this advantage, and its stock value is going to reflect that.

The P/E ratios for many private companies average from 30 percent to 60 percent lower than those for similar publicly held firms. It might be safe to say that if K mart stock were trading at a P/E multiple of 16, a fair price to pay for a privately held retailer of discount general merchandise would be from 6 to 11 times its current adjusted net income.

Is the P/E pricing method ironclad? Of course not. The price of a company is ultimately set by the agreement of a willing buyer and a seller who wishes to sell. But the P/E ratio makes for a powerful argument in price negotiations.

Learn from Research

The effort put into researching a particular industry and company, if done patiently and thoroughly, will yield much more than general knowledge of that industry. It will open the researcher's eyes to some of the intricacies of the business the acquirer is considering.

A diligent researcher will learn the philosophies and plans

that are being followed by companies in the intended market. Just as importantly, some of the unsuccessful plans will be unearthed as well. Better yet, an untapped corner of the market might be discovered.

An acquirer should come away from the evaluation process enthused and excited about the company and the industry that has been evaluated. If facts and intuition lead an acquirer to believe that the target company is in the wrong kind of business, it's best to step back and reassess the whole acquisition plan.

The people who succeed will be objective and honest with themselves. If you are undecided, it is wise to ask for a third party opinion. But if you are excited and enthusiastic at this point, and can't wait to close the deal, then you're ready for the next step.

NEGOTIATIONS: STRATEGY AND TACTICS

Contact the seller and set up another meeting. At least an hour will be needed. A place where all can sit and talk in confidence is an essential ingredient. If the seller asks about bringing an attorney or accountant, say that you don't think that's necessary. Your own attorney and accountant will not attend the meeting; and your objective is simply to learn a little more about the business.

It's often best to get the seller out of his place of business for this meeting, because of the fear of being overheard or interrupted. It's best if you can agree on an environment that will allow the seller to concentrate on your discussions and be completely candid.

The Buyer's Objectives and Strategy

The objectives for this meeting are simple and straightforward: Learn the seller's *real* reason for selling. Then, begin serious discussion of price and terms. Although these are delicate things to discuss, they are the basis for creating any deal. It's important to use the best psychological approach. Be well-prepared for this meeting; know what to say and how to say it.

How to Conduct the Meeting

At the meeting, exchange pleasantries, get coffee or soft drinks, and make everyone comfortable. Get down to business fairly quickly. The seller will be anxious, and possibly nervous, so don't keep him in suspense too long.

Open the meeting by confirming an interest in his company, and ask him to tell how he got started in business—how it all began. This will relax him and get him talking about something he probably loves to talk about. Listen patiently, and be sure not to sidetrack his story.

Let him bring the story right up to date, then step in and say "And I guess that brings us up to the present. After all the time and work you've put into the business, it must be a big decision to sell. I wonder ... What are your personal objectives?" *Listen carefully to his response.* If he doesn't seem to have any specific plans, or if he contradicts something he's told you earlier, beware of his stated motive for selling.

People who sell healthy companies don't make spur-of-the-moment decisions, and they usually aren't pressed for time. But if an owner decides that he needs to unload his company because it's deteriorating, then he will have only one thing in mind: Get rid of the company fast! He won't have spent months or years planning his next venture or what he'll be doing during his retirement.

Gather Intelligence by Listening.   If the explanation of why he's selling and what he plans to do after he sells is satisfactory, the seller's plans provide additional information you can use: If he plans on starting a new venture, or he wants to work or consult with other companies, you will need a strong noncompetition clause as a condition of the sale. If he plans to retire completely and take up some hobbies or travel, then there's a good chance that he won't need a large amount of cash up front. Payments stretched out over a period of time might appeal to him.

If you listen carefully to the seller, the information gleaned may be used to your advantage when the negotiation stage is reached.

The Topic of Price.   The last topic to cover in this meeting is money. The seller, in almost all instances, has decided upon an asking price for the business. Sometimes this price is reasonable; often it is not.

You may have noticed, up to this point, that little has been said about the subject of price. There is a reason for that: If you decide you want to buy, and a seller sincerely wants to sell, then price itself will probably not stand in the way.

Price is not the most important consideration when buying a business, surprising as that may sound. Therefore, don't be too concerned about price until this stage of the process is reached.

In doing your research, the stock market's current valuations of public companies similar to that of the acquisition candidate have been determined. You will probably have already applied the P/E pricing formula to the company being considered. More likely than not, the asking price is higher than the price calculated by the P/E method. This arms you with some good, solid ammunition, but don't give the seller your actual calculated price yet.

Tactics for Dealing with Price.   Start the next part of the discussion by telling the seller about the research that has been done on the current selling prices of companies in the same industry. This research has shown that his asking price is somewhat high. Be vague. *Do not tell the seller the price you feel is fair, and do not tell him exactly how high you think his price is.*

Sellers seldom expect to receive the asking price for their business. It's likely that the seller has already calculated what price would be acceptable to him. Knowing this, you should be somewhat forward and say something like, "Look, I'm sure you've already sat down and figured out how much you actually think you'll get for the company. I know that you and I are expected to play these negotiation games. But rather than taking a lot of time going back and forth on negotiations, and spending more money than we need to on accountants and attorneys, why don't we be more up front with each other. If you'll give me the lowest figure you'd be happy with, I'll be honest and tell you if we can make a deal or not."

If there are two or more sellers involved, offer to let them talk in private for a few minutes before answering. But be sure to get a *specific* number from them.

He might say (with a smile on his face) "The asking price." If he does, just smile right back and tell him that you really do want to bypass all the haggling over price. Repeat the question. In all but a few instances, a new and lower price will be quoted by the seller. When he gives that price, thank him and jot it down on a notepad. If it sounds anything close to what might be considered reasonable, tell him you "think something can be worked out."

Whatever Happens, Don't Argue, Complain, or Negotiate. Negotiation can come at a later date. The intention has been to get a price to work with, and that's been accomplished. Whatever the price, its significance will diminish (to you, if not to the seller) as the deal progresses.

For now, the seller has provided what you wanted—a price which is probably significantly below the asking price. The seller no doubt expects you to come back with a lower offer, despite the talk about not wanting to haggle. You, however, should leave the subject alone until the next meeting. For now, there are other things to accomplish.

Determine Minimum Income. It is imperative that the seller verbally commits to a *minimum* pretax income that the business can be expected to earn in the future. This number will become very important as you proceed with the negotiations.

The best way to obtain the above verbal commitment is to approach this matter in a friendly, casual manner. You might find it effective to say, "Mr. Seller, you have shown me that your business can be expected to earn between $300,000 and $400,000 [use actual figures] per year. Is the $300,000 the least I should expect? [He'll probably say yes.] Then, Mr. Seller, if I use a number of half that—$150,000—for my financial purposes, I will be more than safe, won't I?"

The seller, in order to justify his price for the business, has very likely been telling you what a wonderful, profitable business it is. Now he has been asked if it would be safe to use a very conservative number—*half* his stated, or adjusted, figures—for your own conservative financial projections. Naturally, he's going to have to agree that this would be extremely safe.

Make it a point to write this number down on a notepad, adding date, time, place, and attendees at this meeting.

How Much Cash? Ask the seller directly, "How much of that price do you need to have in cash?" The answer will probably be, again with a smile, "All of it!" But keep insisting that it's imperative to negotiate part of the purchase price on payments. Ask again how much cash he needs at closing. The seller will probably mention an acceptable figure, or at least come close. But if the seller insists that the entire price be paid in cash, then some decision making must be done on the spot.

If the company simply doesn't make sense as an all cash purchase, especially at the price quoted, *tell* the seller that the deal can't be justified without better terms. If he doesn't relent, begin gathering notes and papers, telling him it's useless to continue unless he can be more reasonable. If he still doesn't relent, leave on pleasant terms. Be very polite and don't offend his ego, and perhaps he'll change his mind once he's had time to reflect.

What Has Been Accomplished up to Now?

Think about what is going through his mind right now. The seller is probably thinking, "Here is a serious buyer. He's done his homework and has a pretty good idea what companies in this industry are worth. He didn't balk at the price, but he obviously will not pay me all cash." The seller knows that he may lose a bona fide buyer if he doesn't compromise a bit. If he has ever considered taking anything other than all cash, you will find out now. If not, it is time to bow out and go on to the next acquisition candidate.

The only time to seriously consider an all cash deal is when the price is very much below the value you have established for the company.

Complete the Intelligence Gathering

A buyer should leave the meeting with information on several very important points:

1. The seller's plans for the future, after the business has been sold.
2. The real reasons he has decided to sell.
3. The price he'd be happy with, and the amount of that he wants in cash.
4. The minimum net income that can be anticipated from the business, by the seller's own claims.

MAKING THE OFFER

By this point in the process, you should know whether or not you want to buy the business. If the decision is to proceed, the next step will be to make an offer.

This is where the inexperienced purchaser, often at the recommendation of an adviser, will prepare a document known as an "Agreement for Purchase and Sale." This is a legal contract and must be prepared by an attorney.

Attorney's fees for this legal contract may range from $2,500 to $5,000 or more. You would be better advised to keep your money for the time being and, at least for now, forget the Agreement for Purchase and Sale.

Letter of Intent

Since the odds are still against closing the deal, buyer and seller should agree on mutually acceptable terms before incurring large professional fees. The best way to accomplish this is to prepare a nonbinding document known as a *Letter of Intent* (LOI).

You can prepare an LOI on your own. Write the first draft, type it, and then show it to an attorney for legal input. It isn't a binding legal document (if written correctly), and a binding legal contract is not needed just yet.

What Is It?
A Letter of Intent is an informal letter from buyer to seller, stating clearly and simply the terms of the offer. It is not legally binding, but it *is* evidence that both have agreed to certain points. The LOI is brief—generally one or two pages in length. Form is not as important as content. (A sample LOI is included in Appendix D.)

Why Use It?
One of the advantages of a Letter of Intent is that it isn't presented, discussed, or negotiated in the pressurized and adversarial conditions of an actual contract. An LOI isn't normally presented in the presence of the seller's attorneys or advisers. Rather, it is best to arrange a private meeting with the seller, to present the LOI and explain it personally.

Let the seller know that your lawyers and accountants will not be attending the informal meeting. Assure him that he will not be asked to sign anything. If he asks that the LOI be sent to him for a review before the meeting, politely decline the request.

Present and Explain the LOI

Arrange the meeting in a neutral and informal environment where there are other people around, perhaps at a restaurant at lunchtime. Hand the seller the original of the Letter of Intent, already signed and dated, and keep a copy in hand. Suggest that it be read through completely before discussing any of the individual points. Then, when the seller has finished reading it, go over each point, explaining them briefly one by one.

Item #1: Price. The first item in the LOI should be the price of the business. During a previous meeting with the seller, he stated his best price. If that was somewhat reasonable, and the advice was heeded about not haggling over the price, then the best price figure should be used in the LOI. Don't be alarmed at the possibility of overpaying—this amount *won't* be paid when all is said and done.

By beginning the LOI with an agreement to pay the seller's asking price, you accomplish an important psychological objective: the seller is caught off guard. He never expected to see that number in the initial offer. (The amount he had quoted as his best price was actually somewhat higher than he really would have accepted.)

Now he thinks he's won the game, so to speak. He is already mentally counting his money and picturing himself *out* of the business and you *in* it. In reality, however, you have won a crucial strategic point by giving the seller what he thinks he wanted. It will soon be evident that price isn't everything.

Items #2 and #3: Relatively Insignificant.   To give the seller time to catch his breath after being startled by the price, make items two and three comparatively insignificant. Use any two of the following statements.

1. Each party will pay his own legal costs.
2. An Agreement for Purchase and Sale will be prepared, to the satisfaction of both parties, prior to closing.
3. Acceptable employment contracts will be negotiated for key employees.
4. The closing date for the transaction will be between 60 and 90 days after the Agreement for Purchase and Sale is executed.
5. A cash deposit will be made at the time that the Agreement for Purchase and Sale is executed.

Choose two of these five statements for points number two and three, and intersperse the other three among the remaining conditions of the LOI.

Item #4: Cash for Net Worth.   The next key point to include derives from what the authors have labeled the *Cash for Net Worth* rule. This rule isn't found in any other books on business, finance, or mergers and acquisitions. The rule simply states that cash should be paid only for the net asset value of the company—its assets less its liabilities and debts.

Everything that is paid for the business *over* the net asset value is for *future earnings*. If future earnings materialize, as the seller has assured that they will, you will be happy to pay the premium. But any premium should be paid *as the earnings materialize*, not as a cash payment at closing.

This is addressed in the LOI by the following statement: "The cash portion of the purchase price to be paid at closing will be an amount equal to the audited net worth of the company as of that date." Note the word *audited*. You may choose to waive that requirement, but you do so at a certain risk. You should do so only if certain that the seller's Balance Sheet contains accurate figures.

Be wary of the seller who insists there be no audit. This may well indicate that the financial statements are misstated.

Item #5: Minimum Net Worth at Closing.   To protect yourself from the sale of assets of the company prior to closing (you may be counting on these assets to collateralize or secure bank borrowings), include a statement similar to this in the LOI: "The net worth of the company at the time of closing shall be a minimum of $XXX." This minimum should be something fairly close to the company's net worth on the statements shown to the buyer and analyzed by the buyer and his CPA.

(The remaining items in the LOI may be presented in any convenient order. See Appendix D for a sample LOI.)

Seller Financing.   A cash down payment has been offered to the seller that is no more than the net asset value of the company. You have also tentatively agreed to pay the seller's asking price. What about the difference between these two amounts? You are asking the seller to finance the balance.

It's important to realize that the difference between selling price and net asset value can be very significant. The cash part of the sale may be only a small fraction of the total price. Financing this difference is often accomplished by the seller's taking a promissory note from the buyer.

The problem with this approach is that the Balance Sheet of the business being bought becomes loaded with debt at closing.

This makes it difficult or impossible to get traditional bank financing for working capital the business might need. But what alternative is there to traditional debt, if the seller is to receive both the balance of the sales price in installment payments *and* interest on the unpaid balance?

Redeemable Preferred Stock. One potential solution involves the use of a special type of debt-like stock called *Redeemable Preferred Stock.* Any of a number of different types of preferred stock can be issued by a corporation, each with special attributes setting it apart from ordinary common stock. The type of preferred stock that is recommended—redeemable preferred—pays annual dividends and is redeemable, meaning it can be cashed in by the holder at some point in the future. Be sure your lawyer is familiar with this stock.

Let's assume for the moment that a new or surviving corporation controlled by the buyer issues preferred stock to the seller. The amount issued is at a stated value that equals the difference between the sales price of the business and the cash downpayment.

The buyer agrees to pay dividends on the preferred stock at the rate of 10 percent (or another negotiated rate) of the stated value per year. The buyer also gives the seller the right to redeem a certain portion of the stock each year for cash. Redemptions over a five-year period, for example, will have given the seller the total stated value of the stock in cash.

By the end of those five years, the seller will have been paid the total amount of the difference owed him on the purchase price. He also will have received the equivalent of interest, in the form of dividends, on the money owed. Doesn't that sound a lot like a standard promissory note?

In fact, from the seller's point of view, there is little difference between this type of preferred stock financing and standard debt. The important differences are that dividends can be restricted—*paid only if the company earns a profit*—and that the assets of the company aren't available as security to assure redemption of the preferred stock. But the preferred stock will be given preferential treatment over the common stock of the company. If the worst happened, and the company were liqui-

TABLE 6–2
Seller's Balance Sheet

Assets	
Assets	
Current assets:	
Cash	$ 30,000
Inventory	120,000
Equipment (less depreciation)	150,000
Total assets	$300,000
Liabilities and Equity	
Liabilities	
Accounts payable	$ 20,000
Note payable to bank	80,000
Total liabilities	100,000
Equity	
Common stock	20,000
Retained earnings	180,000
Total equity	200,000
Total liabilities & equity	$300,000

dated, the preferred stockholder would get money back before any went to the common stockholders.

So, from the seller's perspective, the preferred stock financing is almost the same as a normal unsecured loan. But there is a tremendous difference between the two *to the buyer*: The redeemable preferred stock, if issued correctly, is shown as *equity* on your new corporation's Balance Sheet, *not as debt*. This allows *much* more flexibility for additional financing, as the only debt shown on the acquiring company's books is the debt assumed from the seller's company.

Your corporate Balance Sheet will also reflect an asset called *goodwill*. This will be the excess of the total purchase price less the net value of the assets that were bought—the same amount that you so creatively financed. This makes your debt-to-equity ratio *very* impressive to bankers or other traditional lenders. This may allow you to borrow most or all of the money needed for the cash down payment on the acquisition.

As further illustration, assume you acquire the corporation whose Balance Sheet is shown in Table 6–2.

Your agreement with the seller is for a total purchase price of $600,000. This will be paid by $200,000 in cash (the value of the company's assets of $300,000 less its liabilities of $100,000—our "cash for net worth" rule) and redeemable preferred stock in the amount of $400,000.

To simplify this example, let's assume that the market value of the equipment the company owns is exactly the same as its depreciated value on the books.

The debt-to-equity ratio for the seller's corporation is 1:2 ($100,000 in liabilities to $200,000 in equity). In other words, it looks like the company owes $1 for every $2 it owns. Not bad, but it could be better.

Now let's look at Table 6–3, which shows the corporation Balance Sheet as it would appear *after* the acquisition. Notice

TABLE 6–3
Post-Acquisition Balance Sheet

Assets	
Assets	
Current assets:	
Cash	$ 30,000
Inventory	120,000
Equipment	150,000
Goodwill	400,000
Total assets	$700,000
Liabilities and Equity	
Liabilities	
Accounts payable	$ 20,000
Note payable to bank	80,000
Total liabilities	100,000
Equity	
Common stock	200,000
Preferred stock	400,000
Total equity	600,000
Total liabilities & equity	$700,000

the treatment of the $400,000 worth of preferred stock (the premium paid for the business over the net value of its assets); it is carried as an asset called goodwill. This has caused the debt-to-equity ratio to improve from 1:2 to 1:6 ($100,000 in liabilities to $600,000 in equity, including the $400,000 in preferred stock).

A banker will read this as meaning there is $6 invested in the company for every $1 of debt. That's an admirable ratio for *any* company. Through this one maneuver, a buyer has converted seller financing into a genuine asset on the financial statements. *That's* creative financing!

A Note on the Dividend Rate to Offer. The dividend rate to offer on the preferred stock is a matter for negotiation, of course. The seller is probably going to want it to be a little better than current interest rates on corporate bonds of public companies. An initial offer at a rate perhaps two percentage points under what can be actually paid is appropriate.

Tie Earnings into Redemption Schedule. So far, a buyer will have done well by using this preferred stock "financing" arrangement. But it's not over yet: There is one additional curve a buyer can throw.

Be assured that the seller, during his sales pitch, will have claimed again and again that net profits "will be at least XXX dollars" per year. In fact—in our example earlier—you got the seller to commit to a conservative minimum profit level in your negotiations. He's painted himself into a corner on this figure, and now's the time to take advantage of the situation.

Rather than redeeming a *fixed amount* of the preferred stock each quarter (or each year), offer to cash the seller out based on the minimum profit level he has assured you the company will earn.

For example, if the seller had consistently claimed that the business would earn *at least* $150,000 per year, then a buyer might offer to apply 50 percent (a negotiable item) of any profits above $60,000 per year toward the redemption. This is the way it would work: If the company earned $150,000 in the next year, then $45,000 worth of the preferred stock would be redeemed

($150,000 less $60,000, times 50 percent). But if the company earned $250,000, then $95,000 would be retired. The seller is quickly rewarded if the business does as well as he represented it would do.

Cash Flow Must Be Considered. Before making *any* offers regarding redemption payments, however, (or even about normal debt payments), it's *imperative* that you work with your accountant to calculate cash flow in the new business. The cash generated from the business may be much less than the profits that are projected, even though the business achieves those projections. For this reason, it's critical that you get professional help in calculating cash flow at different levels of profitability. Then make a redemption offer on the basis of what the business can *safely afford to* pay.

Benefits to Seller. The important thing to remember about using Redeemable Preferred Stock is that, from the seller's perspective, the deal differs little from one involving "normal" unsecured financing. If the business does as well as he says it *can* do, then he'll be repaid even more quickly than would be the case with a standard promissory note. And you will have acquired a company that is easy to finance.

Do all deals go this smoothly, with the sellers accepting Redeemable Preferred Stock for the total balance due on their business? Of course not. But many do. And many others can be negotiated with some combination of the preferred stock and traditional debt. Experience has shown that the less experienced and sophisticated the sellers, the more difficulty there is in convincing them to take the redeemable stock.

But, certainly, the greater the percentage of cash or traditional debt the buyer must pay, the less should be paid for the business in total. All these concepts are merely tools to use in overall negotiations.

Key Employees. The Letter of Intent should also cover the obligation of the seller and the key employees to stay with the business during the transition. Very often, especially in smaller businesses, the success of a company has been built on the strengths, abilities, and contacts of its owner or several of its key employees. If this is the case with the company being acquired, then it's extremely important that these people be obligated to remain with the company for a while. The current owner may not want to be bound for a period longer than a few weeks or months. Other key employees need to be willing to stay with the company for longer periods of time—at least a year. This should be addressed in the LOI by the statement, "The seller will agree to remain with the company in a management/consultant position on a full-time basis for at least two months after closing. All key management employees will agree to employment contracts for a period of at least one year."

Non-Compete Agreement. A related clause in the LOI, and a very common one in all business buy-sell agreements, is a non-compete clause. This prevents the seller from moving nearby and opening an identical or similar business—and stealing many of your customers in the process.

The non-compete agreement itself might be drafted separately or as part of the Agreement for Purchase and Sale. It will limit the seller's future competition to a particular geographic region and to a particular period of time (perhaps five years). Without specific limitations, a buyer would have problems defending the agreement in court. Don't worry about these limitations for the LOI. The main thing is to have the seller agree in spirit to a general noncompetition arrangement.

After the seller has looked over the LOI, explain that he should take his time thinking about it and responding (within the 10-day period you've specified, naturally). He may want to negotiate a little over lunch, and there's no harm in that. But he needs to give careful thought to each point, and that's going to take some time.

Tell him to call anytime, either to answer questions that might come up, or to set up another meeting. Expect the seller to phone several times before he's actually ready to meet again. He'll probably want to clarify some things and have others re-explained. Expect him to modify, or even rewrite, the LOI. Meet with him to discuss these changes—let *him* explain them—and try to reach acceptable compromises.

Don't become overanxious! Let the negotiations proceed at their own pace. Don't be afraid to walk away from the deal if the seller is being unreasonable. *Never* be coerced into terms or conditions you're uncomfortable with; you're better off dropping the whole deal and starting over somewhere else. *Never* be afraid to do that.

CLOSING THE DEAL

After the Letter of Intent has been signed by both parties and the major terms of the deal agreed upon, it is time to put these terms into binding legal language. This is the time to begin creating the Agreement for Purchase and Sale. It is critical to use an attorney who is experienced in purchase and sale agreements. An inexperienced attorney should not learn this specialized segment of law at your expense.

The Agreement for Purchase and Sale

The terms and conditions that were negotiated and agreed upon in the LOI stage should be preserved in the first draft of the Agreement for Purchase and Sale (the "contract"). To do anything else would ruin your credibility with the seller. Instruct the attorney that he or she is *not* to produce a standard contract off a word processor and present it to the seller as the first draft, but is to include *each* and *every* specific provision covered by the LOI.

When the first draft is completed, it should be read carefully to be sure it includes wording that describes everything already agreed upon with the seller. Take time reading the contract and make notes where you feel that there should be changes, better descriptions, definitions, or deletions. If you don't understand what some particular section means, then the seller isn't going to understand it either. Don't be afraid to ask the attorney to reword a section for clarity.

Most attorneys will probably include several "gimmies"— minor conditions that are included only so that some concessions can be made during the contract negotiations. Supposedly, even minor concessions make the other party feel he is getting cooperation in making the deal. In reality, an experienced attorney will spot most of these "gimmies" and recognize them for what they are. Nevertheless, this is a common practice in the legal profession, so go along with them as long as the conditions don't conflict with something already established in the LOI.

When you are satisfied that the first draft is accurate and complete, have the attorney send it, unsigned, directly to the seller's attorney. The seller will be notified by his attorney when it has been received. They'll meet to go over it, line by line, making notes and suggested modifications. Then they'll notify your attorney that they're ready to go over the contract.

This first meeting between buyer and seller and their attorneys should accomplish several things: clarify certain points in the contract; change wording where there is no disagreement; and, most importantly, let you find out where the big problems lie—the remaining negotiating points. Don't expect to finalize the contract at this meeting (we've never seen it happen). Just try to come to final agreement on as many of the points as possible.

The best way to reach agreement on a good number of points is to go through the contract page by page, in order, marking the wording of the sections where the other party has problems. *Don't stop to discuss and negotiate each of the problems.* Simply say, "OK, we'll come back to that later."

After going through the entire contract, everyone will probably find that there isn't sufficient time or energy to go back to the problem areas at this first meeting. At least two or three hours will have been used in the review process, and everyone will be tired. It's *not* a good idea to negotiate problems when tired. The wisest thing is to adjourn the meeting for a couple of days, so that both sides have a chance to relax and think about the potential problems from a fresh point of view.

It's best to arrange the next meeting before leaving the first one. That keeps the enthusiasm high, and keeps minor points from being forgotten.

Prior to the Second Meeting

While waiting for the next contract session, your attorney will revise the agreement to reflect the items agreed upon at the first meeting. Have this revised version delivered to the seller's attorney. At the same time, meet with your attorney to discuss the areas of disagreement. Point out where there might be compromises. Also determine which points are the "deal breakers."

Persist until Both Sides Agree

Meet with the seller and his attorney as often as necessary, and be well prepared for each of these meetings. When all the points are agreed upon and the contract is satisfactory to both parties, it is time to sign the agreement and make the deposit.

The Deposit

Every seller is going to insist upon a deposit. Most will want it to be a substantial one. The amount and timing of this deposit will be one of the terms to be negotiated, preferably in the LOI.

Sellers will insist that a large deposit shows good faith. This is nonsense! Most of the very largest deals in the business world today go to contract and close without any deposit at all. Why? Because a deposit doesn't reflect anywhere near the commitment that is evidenced by the value of the time expended on research and negotiation—plus the thousands of dollars already spent on professional fees.

It is not wise to tie up substantial amounts of money which provide no financial benefit to the buyer or seller—it is not an efficient use of funds. But the fact remains that the seller will want a deposit to validate the contract. Ironically, the smaller the deal the more problems that are likely to be encountered in negotiating this point. Ideally, the deposit should be limited to a token amount. A good compromise would be for the buyer to deposit $5,000 *into the escrow account of the buyer's attorney*.

Sign the Agreement

If all goes well, the day will finally arrive when all the parties involved will meet to sign the Agreement for Purchase and Sale. This is not the closing, though. Just like buying a house, the actual closing takes place at a specified time after the contract is executed.

The period of time between signing and closing should be *at least* 60 days. You will have a great deal to accomplish. If the closing is contingent upon a satisfactory audit, you will need to have the accountants get started on their examination at once. Financing may need to be arranged either to help with the cash portion of the purchase price or to provide a line of credit for the business once it is taken over. The buyer will also need to have a new corporation created for the transferred business, if that's the form chosen.

Commonly Overlooked Tasks

The two most commonly overlooked jobs that a buyer should be doing during the period between signing and closing are:

1. *The creation or refinement of a business plan.* The business plan will establish direction for the business and will identify the goals that the new ownership intends to achieve.
2. *Making a plan for the transition period* from the seller's business to the buyer's business. This plan will define the tactics to be used, immediately following the closing, to establish the new owner with the employees, customers, and suppliers.

The Transition Plan

Each employee, customer, and supplier is going to wonder and speculate about the new owner. What new plans are intended for the company? What kind of person is the buyer? How will the relationship with the company be affected? It's imperative that a new owner answer these questions as soon as possible.

Deal with these people as *individuals*. Speak with each privately, informing them of plans, philosophy, and business goals. Listen to what these people say, for there is a tremendous amount to be learned from them. Ask each person what he or she likes most about the company as it now exists. Ask employees if there is anything they can think of that would improve their ability to do their job. Ask if there's anything about the company that they *don't* like, and what could be changed to make it better. Take notes during these discussions, because it's going to be impossible to remember everything, especially during the hectic transition phase.

This thoughtful and insightful approach—asking for the input of everyone involved with the company—earns a new owner a big supply of goodwill. The employees, customers, and suppliers will believe that the new boss genuinely cares about what *they* think.

Closing Day

On the day of the actual closing, expect to spend an entire morning or afternoon going over the agreement and documentation. If lenders are involved in the closing, begin the meeting early in the morning. Approval for certain items may be required, and if it's 6:00 P.M. before such a need is discovered, it's unlikely that the senior bank officers will be in their offices when needed. Also, avoid closings on Fridays because of the chance that delays might push the final signing to a Monday or Tuesday.

When the papers are signed and the money changes hands, there will be a collective sigh of relief from everyone involved. Not every transaction makes it all the way to closing. Enjoy the euphoric feelings, and celebrate if you have any energy left. Both the buyer and seller will remember this ordeal for the rest of their lives, and will cherish the feeling of accomplishment. Tomorrow you will have your work cut out for you—you have a business to run!

CHAPTER 7

TAKING YOUR
COMPANY PUBLIC

---

*A mysterious and sophisticated process
simplified and clearly explained*

In This Chapter:

GOING PUBLIC: WHAT DOES IT MEAN?

Anyone who has read magazines or newspapers or who has watched the business news on television has seen or heard the term "going public." In strictly a news sense, "going public" means telling the world something for the first time. In a business sense, "going public" means that a company has decided to sell an ownership interest to the general public for the first time.

A company going public does so through an "initial public offering" or IPO. This IPO can be arranged through a qualified stockbrokerage firm known as an underwriter (or investment banker, or broker-dealer—all these terms mean about the same thing). An IPO can also be conducted by the company itself through what is known as "self-underwriting."

After a company goes public—that is, once it has completed its initial public offering—it is partially or wholly owned by investors. To protect these stockholders and inform them of developments and conditions in the now-public company, certain disclosures are required.

The Securities and Exchange Commission (SEC) mandates that material facts and financial information be disclosed by the company. This disclosure is required at the time of its IPO and thereafter on a regular basis. Financial statements must be audited on at least an annual basis. Annual reports on the general condition of the business must be filed with the SEC and sent to shareholders. Any major changes in the business in ownership or control also trigger reports. Laws requiring these reports were written in the 1930s after the stock market crash of 1929.

Once a company goes public, it has no direct control over the price of its stock. Rather, the price is established by buyers and sellers negotiating with one another in what is known as an "auction" market. Prices offered by the sellers (the "offers") and by the buyers (the "bids") are known to each other and to all interested parties. As often as not, the company whose stock is being traded has no more knowledge than the average investor of why its stock moves up or down.

Shares of stock can be traded in several ways. There are the organized markets, or "exchanges," including the New York Stock Exchange (NYSE), the American Stock Exchange (AMEX), and the Pacific Stock Exchange. There are also the informal over-the-counter market (OTC) and the automated OTC National Association of Securities Dealers Automated Quotations System, commonly known as NASDAQ (pronounced "naz-dak"). The formal systems, including NASDAQ, have certain "listing requirements." These requirements govern such things as the number of shareholders and the amount of assets a company must have in order to be traded on the exchange (or be "listed").

WHY GO PUBLIC?

There are a number of pros and cons to consider before deciding to go public. Here are some of the negative points that argue against such a decision:

Negative Point #1: Life in a Fishbowl
The management of a public company must answer to shareholders, the SEC, its auditors, and the investment community in general, including analysts and reporters. There is almost always someone second-guessing management's decisions and strategy. This continual questioning is unattractive to entrepreneurs who have run companies with no one to answer to but themselves.

Negative Point #2: Reporting and Paperwork
Audited financial statements are required by the SEC. Audits can be expensive, ranging from about $20,000 for smaller companies into the millions for large public companies. In addition, many other reports must be filed with the state and federal agencies that oversee publicly held companies. These reports are time-consuming and costly to produce.

Negative Point #3: Loss of Control
It is often necessary to relinquish control of a company when it is taken public. An owner who formerly answered to no one must suddenly bear responsibility for acts and decisions that would otherwise have been a private matter. The founder of a company can find himself pushed out by the company's board of directors. This is what happened to Steve Jobs and Steve Wozniak, the celebrated founders of Apple Computers. They are no longer affiliated with the company they started.

Negative Point #4: Limited Pay, Benefits, and Perquisites

Owners of privately held companies can pretty much do as they please when it comes to salaries and benefits for themselves.

If the boss wants a company plane or a private limousine or a secluded retreat in the mountains, the decision is totally his or hers. But in a company whose stock is held by outsiders— the general public—some of the shareholders might object to corporate funds being spent to pad the egos of management.

There are other reasons why some owners of private companies prefer to keep their companies private, but these are the most common. As in most cases, however, there are two sides to this coin. There are certainly many good reasons to take a company public. Here are a few:

Positive Point #1: Wealth Creation

Simply put, this is *reason number one* for going public. We all have read the stories about young Bill Gates of Microsoft, whose stockholdings in the computer software company he founded are worth around a billion dollars. Would Bill's stock be worth that much if his company were still privately held? Of course not. A company that is publicly held, especially a rapid growth company such as Microsoft, gets much of its value from the enthusiasm the public holds for its future earnings potential. There are exceptions, of course, but a publicly held company will generally be valued much higher than a similar private company.

Positive Point #2: Liquidity

Owners of private companies may have difficulty selling their ownership interests even if a specific value can be established for the stock. There simply aren't as many interested buyers as if the stock were publicly traded. A potential buyer would likely want control, which would require a substantial investment. This leads to *seller-financing*, with the purchase price being paid over an extended period of time. Publicly traded companies have few of these problems. The general public can buy any number of shares at most any time. The seller of the stock receives payment in just a few days.

Liquidity is also important when trying to get an estate in

order. Frequently, the heirs of a privately held company must sell the entire business in order to obtain the money necessary to pay estate taxes. If a company is publicly held, however, some stock can easily be sold to raise cash. Enough of the stock can be retained to maintain a strong family interest in the company and perhaps even control. The Ford Motor Company did this, raising money for its operations with a public stock offering while retaining family control of the corporation.

Positive Point #3: Specific Valuation
What is the value of a privately held company? Appraisals can be performed for a company just as with real estate. Until an actual buyer is found, the appraisal is really only an estimate of the company's value. Anyone who has tried to obtain bank financing by offering shares in a privately held company as security will have learned what outsiders think of appraisal values—not very much.

Stock in a publicly traded company is a different matter. Its value may change daily, but at least an accurate valuation is readily available at any time.

Positive Point #4: Ease of Raising Capital
Once a company has gone public, it can raise additional capital, usually with greater ease than if it were privately held. This is true not only because of the "specific value" the marketplace gives the company's stock but because there is greater accessibility to funds. Private investors may reach a limit beyond which they will make no additional investments, for either monetary or psychological reasons. The stock market, however, remains nearly insatiable.

Positive Point #5: Flexibility in Making Acquisitions
A private company is usually limited to using hard cash and promissory notes to buy another company. A public company, on the other hand, can negotiate to pay the seller with stock. This stock is liquid and has a specific value to both buyer and seller. Buying with stock can allow a company to conserve its cash and lines of credit for normal business operations.

Many of the large diversified companies of today—

companies such as Gulf & Western Industries—were built by acquiring companies with stock rather than cash.

Positive Point #6: Credibility and Visibility
Publicly held companies normally receive more publicity than all but the largest and most aggressive privately held companies. This recognition factor is sometimes important in helping a firm's credibility with customers, lenders, and the business community. A public company's financial statements, audited and scrutinized by regulators, are readily accepted. This makes it easier for the public company to obtain credit from suppliers and other sources.

The Decision-Making Process

If the time is ripe to take your company public, there are certain decisions that can be made that will reduce the time and frustration normally encountered in the process. The decision-making process deals with many variables. Some are controllable and others aren't. The better the variables involved are understood, the better the resulting decisions will be. An owner will, for example, have to choose an underwriter. The quality and capability of the underwriter will determine the chances of the IPO's ultimate success.

Timing is of paramount importance. If all the factors surrounding an offering are acceptable but the timing is bad, with the stock market in a slump or recession, it is unwise to proceed. With the right market conditions, a company can get a lot: a higher price per share, greater investor interest, and a more active aftermarket.

WHEN SHOULD A COMPANY GO PUBLIC?

There isn't any magic formula that determines when a company is ready for an initial public offering. Two important questions that should be answered are, "Is the market ready?" and "Is the company ready?" If either answer is no, then it should be obvious that it's not time for an IPO.

Is the Market Ready?

Items cannot be sold when there are no buyers. This holds true both for vacation trips to Beirut and for shares in an IPO. The stock market and the economy are constantly in a state of flux. Some times are better than others to go public.

How can you tell if the market is ready? Listen to the market itself. Are other companies comparable to yours going public? Are any companies at all going public? If so, how are these IPOs being received by investors? Does the price of the newly issued stock rise in the aftermarket, or is it weak? All these factors will indicate whether the market timing is good or bad.

It is often said in the real estate business that the three most important factors are location, location, and location. Similarly, the three most important factors in deciding when to go public are timing, timing, and timing.

Is the Company Ready?

Only management, with great objectivity, can decide if the company is ready to go public. A company should have its house in order before it takes such a big step. Business plans should be up to date, as should financial statements.

Preparations should include preliminary interviews with attorneys experienced in SEC law and public offering transactions. Research should be performed on both the stock market and on the status of IPOs of companies comparable to yours.

It's important to recognize that an IPO is something that must be sold—sold first by the company's executives to the underwriters, then by the underwriters to their clients and investors. Learn what the market and the underwriters want *first*, and *only then* contact them about your company as an IPO prospect.

HOW TO FIND AN UNDERWRITER

There are many different types of underwriters. There are many small or regional investment firms that specialize in IPOs for newer or midsize companies, and there are the giants of the industry like Merrill Lynch, Prudential Bache, Shearson Lehman-Hutton, First Boston, Morgan Stanley, and Salomon Brothers.

It's unlikely that any of the behemoths will be interested in taking a company public unless it's already firmly established in its industry, it has proven management, and it has revenues of at least $30 million to $40 million per year.

To determine which of the available underwriters is best for a company, it is necessary to do some intelligence gathering. This research effort should provide the names of underwriters who have recently been involved with IPOs of companies somewhat similar to your IPO candidate.

The place to start is the reference section of the nearest large library. The task is to find a sampling of companies that are as similar to the IPO candidate company as possible. Look in the Standard & Poor's and Dun & Bradstreet corporate directories. The company descriptions in these reference works will indicate which of the companies are publicly held.

Next, find out when each of these companies first went public. Identify the most recent initial offerings. This information can be found in the individual "Stock Reports" issued by Standard & Poors or in *Moody's Corporate Records*, which gives a history of most public companies.

A call to the company's headquarters (request the Corporate Secretary's office) may also be made. Ask for the name of the underwriter who took them public, and ask for a copy of their original prospectus. Also inquire as to whether they have had any recent secondary stock offerings, and ask for a copy of their "Annual Report" and "10-K" Report.

While at the library, visit the periodical room to see if they have copies of the *Investment Dealer's Digest*. This magazine is written and published for those in the investment business. It offers a wealth of information on current stock offerings. It is another source of names in the search for an underwriter, and it can provide other valuable information: the valuation used in each offering, the price of the shares offered, and the percentage of the company offered to the public.

Research the Underwriters Involved

After gathering information on companies similar to the IPO candidate that have gone public recently, call the underwriters involved. Give them names of the specific companies you looked up, and ask for prospectuses on them and also on other companies they have taken public recently.

Get as much information from the underwriters as possible. Ask how their IPOs performed in the "aftermarket"—the open trading market that develops after the IPO is completed. Did most of their new issues rise slightly in the months after they were offered? If so, this generally indicates that the IPO was priced well. Conversely, if their new issues dropped soon after the offering, the issues may have been overpriced.

Consider Pricing and Offering Size

Successful IPOs of companies similar to your candidate company will indicate the percentage of ownership that will have to be sold to the public. This percentage is nearly always a stumbling block between entrepreneurs and underwriters.

The underwriter may feel that 30 percent of the company should be sold in an IPO. The entrepreneur might feel that anything over 10 percent is giving the company away. It is rare that the entrepreneur wins this argument, and for good reason: Underwriters make it their business to know the acceptable range for these percentages. They are involved in these market-sensitive decisions every day. The entrepreneur, on the other hand, probably has only an inkling of what factors are involved in deciding valuation, pricing, and percentage of a company to be sold.

The *market* tells the underwriter *what it will pay* for certain kinds of companies; the price is not actually the underwriter's decision. This is like selling your used car: You might think it's worth a certain amount, but the market for cars of that type actually determines what you can get for it. The underwriter knows, in effect, the "blue book" value for companies like yours. Because the market isn't going to overpay, overpricing will result in an unsold IPO.

Before talking with an underwriter, you need to arm yourself with facts and information. This way, you can prepare a realistic scenario for taking your company public. It's important to have specific plans and ideas for your company. That these plans and ideas should be presented to the interested underwriters in a written business plan should be obvious by now. As we have said elsewhere in this book, attempting to raise money without a written business plan is difficult or impossible, and going public is a form of raising money.

Contacting the Underwriters

The information you've gathered will tell which underwriters have taken companies public that are similar to yours. You've researched those underwriters and have examined the prospectuses of their recent IPOs. You have a good idea of the value and pricing of these companies. And you've come up with a range of values for stock prices and for the percentage of the company to be sold in an IPO. You've done your homework. Now it's time to pick up the phone and make the initial calls to these underwriters.

The Phone Call

Try to make all your calls to targeted underwriters during the same week. This way, you'll be in the right frame of mind and concentrating on the call as a priority. Call in the afternoon, if possible, between 1:30 P.M. and 2:30 P.M. The hectic part of the day is over—mornings are busiest—and the underwriters will be in the best frame of mind to take calls. Ask to speak to the person who handled the such-and-such (use a specific company obtained from your research) offering. This shortcut allows you to move directly to the right person. If that person happens to be out of the office at the time, leave a message. Ask for the best time to call back. Stay in control of the situation—don't leave word to have your call returned.

If you leave a message that contains only your name and not what you're calling about, then an interesting thing happens: The recipient searches his memory to place your name, and when he can't, his curiosity is aroused. When you call again, his first thought is, "Hey, this is that person who called yesterday and didn't leave a number. Let's see who it is." Already you've gotten his attention.

Introduce yourself and tell the underwriter that you have examined the prospectus of PQR Company and watched the stock's performance in the aftermarket. If you feel he did a good job on the offering, tell him. Mention that you've selected him as one of three (or two or four) investment bankers that you are interviewing regarding an IPO for your company.

He'll ask some questions about your company. Get right to the point. The fewer words said, the better. Give him the highlights of the company and the plan for the future, emphasizing the next five years. His interest, if any, should become obvious after only a few minutes. If he has no interest in the proposal, ask him for referrals: "Who do you think would have an interest in a deal like this? Do you mind if I mention that you gave me his name?"

An interested underwriter will ask that you send him the business plan and some information on the company. Send whatever he wants. He will give it his attention.

After mailing the package, call the underwriter to let him know when it was sent. Also tell him when you will be available to answer his questions and explain some of the details.

Not every underwriter you contact is going to have an interest in your company. He or she might give any of a thousand reasons. You'll never be sure of the real one. Just accept it and dial the phone again. Don't get discouraged: Persistence is the name of the game.

If *every* underwriter you contact expresses a lack of interest, then it's time to re-evaluate the marketability of your company and its public offering potential. Maybe it's the market rather than your company, but it's time to be realistic. Whatever the reason for the lack of interest, try to pinpoint it. As the old saying goes, you can't fix what you don't know is broken.

The First Meeting with the Underwriter

If the underwriter agrees your company is ripe to go public and the market is ready for your stock, then the next step is either to visit the underwriter or to have him visit you. This might be your first face-to-face meeting with an underwriter. Prepare for it.

Dress the part of a serious businessperson. Have your key people briefed and available before the meeting takes place. If you are visiting the underwriter's office, make sure your key people are available back at the home office. This way if a question comes up that you can't answer, you can immediately call the person who has that specific information.

The topics covered at this first meeting will vary, but you will be asked for your opinion of what percentage of the company is appropriate to offer to the public. That's like the car salesman asking how much you think your car is worth. The underwriter and the car salesman both expect an unreasonable answer. Surprise the underwriter. Give him a realistic range of figures. Disclose the source of your estimates: Name the companies and quote figures from the underwriter's own prior IPO prospectuses. (Be sure the companies are truly similar to yours. If you're not comparing apples with apples, your credibility will suffer.)

"Yes" or "No"?

By the time the meeting is over, you should know if the underwriter is interested in your company. If he says no, thank him for his time and ask him what might be done to make this a more attractive deal in his eyes. Listen well and, above all, don't argue with him. You can learn some valuable things even from those who turn you down.

If the underwriter decides that he needs more information, or if he wants to visit your premises, be as cooperative as possible without being overbearing. Eventually, he'll tell you if he's interested in being your underwriter.

Starting the IPO Process

The underwriter might ask for a retainer before any work is done. From his viewpoint, asking for a retainer is one way of determining the sincerity and commitment of a potential underwriting client. A retainer also offsets expenses incurred as a result of examining your deal.

But from your viewpoint, a retainer at this point is premature. Key factors have not been negotiated. Without knowing the underwriter's ideas on fair valuation, pricing of the stock, percentage of the company to be sold, or the underwriter's fees and expenses, no company should obligate itself to an underwriter.

The next step should properly be for the underwriter to issue a nonbinding letter of intent. This letter will contain most of the key issues mentioned above and will outline the responsibilities of both parties.

Underwriter's Letter of Intent

The terms of the letter of intent are negotiable. After reading it, don't immediately balk at anything. Digest the whole offer first and then come up with a reasonable counterproposal. If you reach an agreement (you may be negotiating with more than one underwriter at this time, although they won't be too happy about that), it is entirely reasonable for the underwriter to ask for, and receive, a retainer.

How much should the retainer be? The lower the better, but for an offering of under $5 million, a retainer of $25,000 is not unreasonable. The underwriter's legal fees and personnel expenses attributable to the offering will reach that amount quite rapidly. This may seem like a lot of money, but it's only a small part of the total cost of an initial public offering. Fees, costs, and expenses will be discussed later in this chapter.

VALUING A COMPANY FOR A PUBLIC OFFERING

In our chapter on raising money for your business, we discussed an easy-to-use method for placing a value on a company. That same method can be applied, along with information garnered from research into IPOs of comparable companies, to get a reasonable estimate of the value of your company.

If your estimate of value is objectively calculated, there should be only a slight difference in your valuation and the underwriter's. The underwriter will be somewhat more conservative, while the entrepreneur will be more aggressive. The "right number" is probably somewhere in the middle. But it will be closer to the underwriter's estimate than the company's.

In most instances, a final valuation will not be reached until shortly before the registration is approved (on what is called the *effective date*). An upper and lower range of values are normally settled on at an early date. The underwriter won't commit to a specific value because of the time that will elapse before the registration statement becomes effective. During this period, the market could change significantly. In fact, it's not unusual during periods of market unrest to have an offering postponed until the market improves.

When an offering is canceled or postponed, the costs, fees, and other expenses already incurred by the prospective issuer are lost. There is no recourse to recover any of this money unless the offering is reinstated. This is one of the risks inherent in a public offering.

TYPES OF OFFERINGS: "FIRM COMMITMENT" VERSUS "BEST EFFORTS"

There are two basic types of offerings an investment banker can employ when taking a company public: "firm commitment" and "best efforts." The differences are substantial and important.

Firm Commitment

In a firm commitment offering, the underwriter buys every share of stock from the issuer at a negotiated price and then resells these shares to the public. The sale may be made to clients of the underwriter or to a syndicate made up of other broker-dealers or to a combination of the two. There is no risk to the issuer that the public won't buy the stock; the underwriter takes that risk.

Best Efforts

An investment banker offering stock through a best efforts offering doesn't buy the stock from the issuing corporation and then resell it. Rather, he acts as an agent, or "broker," for the company issuing the stock. The investment banker makes its best effort (hence the name) to sell the stock to investors or distribute it through a syndicate. A certain number of shares is established at the beginning of the offer as the minimum number that must be sold. If this minimum isn't reached, then the offering is withdrawn. All the money received from potential investors is returned without deduction.

Which Type of Offering is Better?

Which of these two types of offerings is better for a company considering its initial public offering? Generally, the firm commitment is better because the risk is absorbed by the underwriter. But it is quite difficult to find an underwriter who will take a company public on a firm commitment basis unless the company has impressive revenues and earnings. A small company with sales of $10 million or less should normally not expect to go public on a firm commitment basis. The best efforts offering is the norm for smaller and less seasoned companies.

FEES AND EXPENSES

Professional Fees

Taking a company public is an expensive affair. Attorney fees alone will run at least $25,000 and probably much more than that. Auditor fees will range from $10,000 for a beginning company with very little activity to as much as six figures for a company that has been in business for some time.

Professional fees vary a great deal. The best place to learn what costs to expect is from the prospectuses of companies comparable to yours that have gone public recently. These costs are reported clearly in the prospectuses.

Underwriter's Commission

In addition to professional fees and expenses, the issuer pays the underwriter a fee for taking the company public. This fee is paid in several different ways, all of which are negotiable. The most visible fee is the commission, also called the "gross spread," the "discount," or the "concession." This is simply the difference between the price the issuing company receives for each of its shares and the price that the underwriter sells them for.

In large offerings, the commission normally is 6 to 8 percent of the price the public pays. For smaller offerings, the percentage increases and may range up to 12 percent of the selling price, but it normally hovers around 10 percent. The best indicator, again, is to examine the prospectuses of similar, recent offerings.

Printing

When a company goes public, it must produce a prospectus—the small booklet/brochure that explains the offering to the public. Printing costs of under $15,000 are rare, and most are much higher.

The total cost of going public will vary depending on the size of the offering, the underwriter, the comparative attractiveness of your company, and your negotiating ability.

Table 7–1 from *Venture* magazine (April 1986), lists the costs for the *most expensive* underwriters. It will give you a good idea

TABLE 7–1
The Most Expensive Underwriters

Underwriter	*Average Total Expense as Percentage of Offering	**Average Commissions	Average Deal Size
Venderbilt Securities Inc.	29.1	10.0	$ 469,000
Alpine Securities Corp.	27.2	14.4	260,000
Western Capital & Securities Inc.	25.4	13.2	482,000
Patten Securities	22.7	10.0	1,000,000
Stuart-James Co.	20.9	10.0	2,200,000
Rooney, Pace Inc.	20.1	9.9	4,300,000
Steinberg & Lyman	19.8	10.0	3,600,000
Blinder, Robinson & Co.	19.5	10.0	2,400,000
D. H. Blair & Co.	18.6	9.9	4,800,000
Dillon Securities Inc.	18.5	10.2	852,000

*Includes nonaccountable expenses.
** "Gross Spread" includes underwriters' fees, management fees, selling commisions.

Source: Securities Data Co. Reprinted from *Venture*, April 1986.

of the upper limits for costs when budgeting expenses and commissions for an IPO. *Venture* reported that printing costs in this sample of companies averaged $115,000 and that legal and filing fees ranged from $50,000 to $350,000. Accounting fees fluctuated between $25,000 and $200,000.

Other Forms of Underwriter Compensation

Underwriters have a few other ways to earn extra profits, known in the business as *additional compensation*. You may be able to save money and equity in your company by negotiating these points carefully.

Right of First Refusal—An underwriter generally asks for the right to handle any other stock offering your company may have over the next one or two years. His rationale is that because he was instrumental in taking you public, he should be given the right to work with your company on subsequent offerings. This sounds reasonable until you look at what could happen.

It's possible the underwriter will barely sell the minimum number of shares required to make your offering successful. Personality conflicts may develop with the underwriter's staff. Any number of negative things could happen.

If your company has enjoyed success since its IPO and can attract a better underwriter, why be tied to an exclusive agreement? All things considered, unless you have a history of successful, professional, and pleasant dealings with an underwriter, you should avoid giving a Right of First Refusal. If an underwriter performs well, you will want to do business with him again anyway. But make him *earn* your business; don't give him the *right* to it.

Underwriters' Warrants—It is a common practice for underwriters, especially those who specialize in smaller IPOs, to insist upon receiving warrants as part of their compensation. These warrants give them the right to purchase shares of stock in the future—up to an expiration date one or two years away—at an agreed-upon price.

Underwriters' warrants will be mentioned in many of the prospectuses you gather for research on valuation and costs. They are sometimes granted to the underwriter in the proportion of one warrant for each 10 shares sold by the underwriter on the IPO.

Often, they are exercisable at 120 percent of the original issue price of the stock.

As an example, let's assume that a company offers 1 million shares of stock on its IPO, priced at $1 per share. The issuer sells the underwriter 100,000 warrants (one for each 10 shares sold) at the token price of $100. The warrants are exercisable during the next two years at a price of $1.20 per share.

Let's assume the company is very successful and the stock market is strong. The shares, 18 months later, have reached a price of $8 in the marketplace. Would those 100,000 outstanding warrants still held by your underwriter matter very much to you? Perhaps not, unless you wanted to issue more stock.

Now let's assume the company has grown to where it needs more capital. You begin arrangements to issue an additional 200,000 shares at a price near the current market of $8 per share. Then the underwriter informs you that he will be exercising his warrants. He will buy 100,000 shares for $1.20 per share and then resell them at the same time your company is offering its shares to the public. The underwriter pays $120,000 for the shares, then sells them for $800,000, bringing in $680,000 in gross profit.

But now the 200,000 shares intended to be offered will have to compete with the new 100,000 shares. Suddenly, 50 percent more shares will enter the market. And the proceeds *to your company* for 300,000 shares is reduced by $680,000.

Will this increase in the shares being offered make any real difference? It could if the market for your shares is small. The additional 100,000 shares might oversaturate the market, and the resulting price for the 200,000 new shares might be less than the $8 expected.

Many issuers have the opinion that it does no harm to offer the underwriter warrants as additional incentive. If it's done correctly, we agree. But the underwriter's proposal should be carefully scrutinized before you agree to the deal. Be certain that the exercise of these warrants in the future won't dilute current shareholders' equity too much. The quantities involved should be relatively small when viewed as part of the whole offering.

Consulting Agreements

Another common practice is for an underwriter to negotiate a "financial consulting agreement" with an issuer. This agreement provides for a set monthly fee to be paid for a specified period of time, often up to two years. Ostensibly, the underwriter is paid to advise the client company on financial matters. These matters may include bank borrowing, refinancing of payables and receivables, public or private offerings, and short-term cash investments.

It is rare that a company will receive any services of real value in an arrangement like this. The expertise of small underwriters seldom reaches into the areas of finance that are important to a growing company.

Recognize this monthly retainer for what it really is: additional compensation. Any financial advice a company requires can best be obtained from firms specializing in that particular area. This advice will cost far less than the sum paid to an underwriter whose capabilities and expertise are limited to selling stock.

Nonaccountable Expense Allowance

Underwriters often receive two different types of expense allowances: accountable and nonaccountable. The first type consists of expenses directly related to the public offering, including professional fees, travel, and phone costs. It is normal that an advance is paid to the underwriter out of which some of these expenses are paid. The balance of the underwriter's expenses over the advanced amount is billed to the client company with a detailed accounting of each expense.

The *non*accountable allowance is just that: No detailed accounting is required. This nonaccountable expense allowance is usually limited to about 3 percent of the offering proceeds but can range from 1 to 4 percent. Some of this money does actually go to defray expenses directly incurred in the offering. In many cases, the nonaccountable expense allowance is just what the National Association of Securities Dealers calls it: "additional compensation."

Most companies considering an IPO are unaware that the nonaccountable expense allowance is a negotiable number. Not only is the 3 percent not etched in stone, but the nonaccountable expense allowance doesn't have to be used at all.

HOW LONG WILL IT TAKE TO GO PUBLIC?

There is no quick way to take a company public. The process is time-consuming and sometimes very frustrating. The first step, as discussed in the preceding sections, is to select an underwriter. How long it will take for a particular company to select an underwriter depends mostly on four things:

1. How long it takes to reach the decision to go public.
2. How quickly you can complete the necessary research before meeting with underwriters.
3. How soon you can select an underwriter (or vice versa).
4. How long it takes to reach a tentative agreement on the numbers.

These steps are only the beginning, and there is much more to do before an offering can be successfully completed. We have found a useful timetable in the book *Inside Investment Banking* by Ernest Bloch, published by Dow Jones-Irwin. This timetable has been reprinted (see Appendix E) with the kind permission of Professor Bloch.

How quickly a company can be brought to the point where the timetable begins depends on the speed of your research and negotiations with underwriters and on how prepared the company is for outside inspection. Audited financial statements can take several months to prepare. And a company's existing legal contracts, arrangements with major suppliers, credit agreements, and financing instruments must all be well-documented and ready to pass inspection.

All things considered, an IPO can be accomplished in a matter of a few months if everything goes perfectly, or it can take more than a year if negotiations are slow and problems persist.

WHO BUYS STOCK IN AN IPO?

Most companies going public for the first time spend little time thinking about who they want to own their stock. Many times it makes no difference to them at all as long as *someone* buys it. But it might be an advantage to have certain shareholders.

For example, if the firm going public is an electronic compo-
nents wholesaler that sells to electronics manufacturers, it may
be good to have key people at those manufacturing companies as
investors. Stockholders may send a little extra business your way.

How would the stock get in the hands of these people? Someone probably knows who these key people are and where they
can be contacted. Prepare a list and give it to the underwriter.
His stockbrokers will contact these people. You may even want to
call them yourself. Check with your securities attorney to be sure
there are no problems with doing so.

It may also be an advantage to place stock in as many different hands as possible. Why do this? It helps maintain an active
trading market for the stock. This plan ensures greater liquidity and keeps dealer markups to a minimum. Discuss this strategy with your underwriter. Conversely, if your business is concentrated in a small geographic area, it may be best to keep all the
shareholders within that region.

Another group that could bolster your stock is the institutional investors. These are the pension funds, mutual funds, bank
trust departments, and insurance companies. However, unless
the market value of all your free-trading stock (your "capitalization") is large, these institutional investors probably won't be
interested in investing.

Qualifying as an "institutional" stock lets a company enjoy
the best of a good market, but it can hurt a stock severely in a weak
stock market. The institutional investors tend to drive a stock up
and down with their large buy-and-sell orders.

A company's ability to attract institutional investors will also
depend on the influence its underwriter has with institutional
clients. The possibility of interesting these professional investors
in an IPO stock should be one of the topics discussed with the
underwriters you interview.

"MARKET MAKERS" AND WHY THEY'RE IMPORTANT

"Market makers" are broker-dealers who both offer to buy and
offer to sell shares in a particular company. They are the "wholesalers" of the over-the-counter (OTC) marketplace. They deal in

specific stocks. Regular brokers, on the other hand, act only as agents for their customers when they buy or sell stock. They never actually own the stock themselves.

Some broker-dealers make markets in hundreds of different stocks, while others only make markets in a few. These firms are regulated by the NASD (National Association of Securities Dealers) and are also subject to the rules and jurisdiction of the SEC.

The market makers' profit is made, for the most part, on the difference between what they buy a stock for and what they sell it for. This is known as the "mark-up" or "spread."

As an example, assume a stock is quoted by a market maker at "$10-10^{1}/2$." This means they'll buy at 10 or sell at 10 $^{1}/2$. The spread is $^{1}/2$, or 50 cents per share. As quotes are given for a "round lot"—100 shares—the market maker will buy 100 shares for $1,000 and offer to sell those same shares almost immediately for $1,050, making a profit of $50 on the transaction.

The risk in the above example is that the stock market may move against the broker before the stock can be resold. That's why most market makers try to resell a stock almost immediately.

How can the market maker affect the price of a stock? In the OTC marketplace, where the IPO shares are likely to trade initially, the price of a stock is established by these market makers. The market makers encourage activity in buying and selling because that's how they make a profit. They call their customers and use other aggressive marketing tactics to maintain interest and activity.

The more firms making a market in your stock, the greater the influence on investors to trade in your stock. A high volume of trading usually allows for less fluctuation with large buy-and-sell orders. It also results in a smaller spread between the bid and ask price.

How to Reach the Market Makers

The underwriter should make the initial contacts with the market makers, and the top executives of the company issuing the stock should be available to meet with those who express an interest. Some of these market makers will attend pre-offering meetings arranged by your underwriter (called "due diligence meetings").

At these meetings, your company's executives will talk to groups of professionals from the investment community and discuss your company, its past successes, and its plans for the future.

Many market makers are not only wholesalers of stock but also employ a sales force of stockbrokers who deal with the general public. These stockbrokers, referred to as "retail" men because they retail rather than wholesale stock, are always looking for good ideas for their clients. If a company has a good story behind it, retail brokers have another incentive to recommend the stock: a higher commission if their firm makes a market in the stock.

In general, market makers can help maintain an active, orderly market for a company's stock both in the period immediately following an IPO and in the long term. It will be to your advantage to cultivate them with care.

PUBLICITY AND "DOG AND PONY SHOWS"

There are literally tens of thousands of different stocks competing for investors' attention. Why would a stockbroker recommend that his clients buy *your* stock rather than that of IBM or General Motors? Think about this for a moment, because it's a very real choice that investors must contend with.

There are some very good reasons for investors to buy stock in a smaller company instead of in the "blue chips." You need to be aware of what those reasons are in order to convince the marketplace of your company's merits.

Many investors feel it's wise to diversify their portfolio to include both conservative and aggressive investments. This helps to maximize their profit while retaining a margin of safety. Even staid insurance companies have designated a portion of their portfolios to speculative investments and ventures. So there will be a large group of investors whose objectives include speculative investments. It's just a matter of convincing these investors that the speculative stock they buy should be *yours*.

The first thing is to let the investment community know you exist. Next, they must be convinced that your company has a good chance of success, growth, and profitability. A publicity campaign can get this message to them. Meeting with members of the investment community all across the country will support the publicity effort.

One of the foremost publicity tools for young companies trying to generate investor interest is the "dog and pony show." This is a tongue-in-cheek term for the presentations given by the management of publicly held companies for the benefit of the investment community. These meetings may not sell products, but they sell your *company* to the investment community.

These presentations will usually last about 45 minutes and are attended by stockbrokers, market makers, analysts, newspaper business reporters, and any other local members of the financial community who might have influence over investors. For most of these people, the stock market is both their job and their favorite hobby, and they always want to know who the next big winner in the stock market is going to be. Maybe your company will be it.

The best public speaker in the presenting company should do the talking. If it's the CEO, that's fine; but it's important to have someone who can retain the attention of the audience while remaining professional and believable. More than just numbers and percentages should be discussed—*events, people,* and *plans for the future* should be major topics. The meetings should be followed up with regular mailings to those who attended, including copies of press releases and announcements.

These dog and pony shows are among the most effective means of getting a company's name into the minds of the investment community, but they are also one of the easiest things for smaller public companies to put off doing. Wise businesspeople discipline themselves to take the time to schedule these shows, and they reap the rewards over a long period of time.

ALTERNATIVES TO AN IPO

A company doesn't necessarily have to go through the process of an initial public offering to become publicly held. An alternative is to merge into another company that is already publicly held. In effect, you are using an existing entity that already has shareholders, outstanding stock, and up-to-date regulatory filings as a vehicle to turn a private company into a public one. This method avoids much of the time and expense of arranging an IPO.

Shells

There's been an increase over recent years in the acquisition of public companies called *shells*. They are called "shells" because they have no ongoing business and few, if any, assets. Sometimes they are companies whose assets have been liquidated, leaving only the corporate body and the shareholders.

Their name may bring the carnival midway to mind, with its old "shell game." In truth, some of the activity these public shells are involved in seems as if it properly belongs on the midway. But many public shell transactions are entirely legitimate and benefit all the parties connected with them. Perhaps the biggest disadvantage in taking a company public through one of these public shells, rather than through a "normal" IPO, is that no money is raised through the shell acquisition. Let's look at an example of this type of transaction.

Mr. Smith is the founder and controlling shareholder of ABC Company, which is privately held. Its annual revenues are $9 million, and it is profitable. Mr. Smith would like to take ABC Company public but hasn't been able to find any underwriters interested in an IPO. Smith does come across a company, however, that is publicly held but has no ongoing business and no significant assets. The other company, Mollusk Industries, wouldn't have any value at all except for the fact that its stock is publicly held and traded. The board of directors of Mollusk is interested in having the company used as a shell.

Smith is assured by an independent valuation consultant that his company, ABC, is worth approximately $4.5 million. He compares this estimate with the value of all the issued and outstanding stock of Mollusk Industries (its "market capitalization"). The Mollusk stock is currently being traded at $.50 per share. There are 1.5 million shares issued (1 million of which are controlled by a group of insiders), so the total value of Mollusk at this time is around $750,000. Mollusk has an additional 8.5 million shares that have been *authorized* but that are unissued.

Smith offers to let Mollusk acquire ABC Company in return for 8.5 million shares of newly issued stock. At ABC's current valuation of $4.5 million, this equates to a value of approximately $.52 per share ($4.5 million divided by 8.5 million shares of stock), which is near the current market value of Mollusk's stock.

The board of directors of Mollusk considers this proposal by looking at what will happen to the value of ABC when it becomes a publicly traded company. They decide that the increased liquidity and exposure the company would then have could cause its value to increase to $6 million or $7 million after the transaction. The insiders, who own 1 million shares, would then own 10 percent of the newly public ABC (out of the total 10 million shares), and the value of their stockholdings would be worth $600,000 or $700,000 rather than the current $500,000.

This indicates a potential gain of 40 percent for the controlling shareholders of Mollusk, with the prospect for further gains if ABC's business grows as planned. They weigh the alternatives and decide to accept Mr. Smith's proposal.

Mr. Smith now owns 85 percent of the stock in a public company that could be worth $6 million or $7 million. The company itself, however, hasn't raised the first dollar of new capital.

Mr. Smith, who is now the controlling shareholder in Mollusk Industries, changes the company's name from Mollusk to ABC Corporation. He consults his professional advisers and the representative of a regional underwriter about a new public offering to raise $2.5 million needed for expansion. They decide on the following steps:

Step 1—Have ABC Corporation initiate a 1-for-5 "reverse stock split," exchanging one share of "new" stock for every five shares currently being held by stockholders. This would reduce the number of issued shares from 10 million to 2 million without changing the dollar value of anyone's holdings. The current trading price of the stock would increase from $.60 to $3 per share.

Step 2—Increase the number of authorized shares of common stock from the post-split 2 million to 20 million.

Step 3—Register an offering of approximately 700,000 shares of common stock at a price of $4 per share, raising a gross amount of $2.8 million. After deducting fees and expenses of approximately 20 percent, this would net around $2.3 million for expansion.

If this strategy is successful, the new ABC Corporation will have its shares publicly traded on an active basis by several good market makers, probably in the $4 range. Smith will still control the company with 63 percent of the issued and outstanding shares. His shares, by the way, will be worth approximately $6.8 million. Remember that several months ago his holdings in ABC Company, then a private company, were worth at best $4.5 million.

This scenario is simplified, of course, and the actual implementation of an acquisition would be much more involved and complicated than what is shown here. In the real world, a "private placement" of restricted stock might have been made to investors prior to the $2.8 million offering by the new ABC Corporation. This private placement would help pay some of the expenses of the new offering plus provide the transitional financing needed for operations until the new stock offering was completed.

The acquisition of a public shell can be a viable alternative to an IPO, especially for a private company that has received no encouragement from underwriters about going public. For a shareholder like Mr. Smith, the advantages usually outweigh the disadvantages. A company that would otherwise be restricted in its ability to raise capital is able to avail itself of the public market.

SOME FINAL THOUGHTS ON GOING PUBLIC

In summary, there is more than one way to take a company public. None is quick and easy. All are time-consuming, expensive, and fairly complicated. All require expert professional guidance.

Several of the points covered thus far merit the emphasis of repetition.

Timing. Timing, timing, timing! If the timing isn't right, then don't attempt to go public. Use the time to position your company for a more positive economic and market environment. It will come.

Objectivity. Be objective when assessing a company's attractiveness as a public offering candidate. If the market tells you there is no interest in comparable companies, then listen. This will avoid a costly and embarrassing mistake.

Research. Careful, intelligent research will lift the veil of mystery on many elements that must be considered by those interested in taking their company public. Knowledge will help to make up for lack of experience.

Negotiate. When working with underwriters, know which items are negotiable and which are not. If you know how to approach them, almost everything is negotiable.

Preparation. Be prepared! This is a good motto for Boy Scouts and a good motto for you, especially when it comes to taking a company public. Prepare the company for a public offering. Prepare yourself for negotiations with underwriters. Prepare your management team for their post-offering responsibilities.

Sell. Sell your company to the underwriters. Sell your terms and conditions in the negotiations. And sell the attractiveness of your stock to the stockbrokers, analysts, market makers, reporters, and investors.

Options. Before making any decision, examine your options. Would you be better off going public, or should you stay private? Is an IPO the best solution, or should you acquire a public shell? Which underwriter can offer the best all-around service? The more options you study and the better informed you are about them, the better your decision will be.

Patience. It takes time to do most things right. Going public is certainly no exception. The SEC cannot be hurried. Don't hurry the decision-making process. There are few shortcuts, and no good ones.

Fairness. The best deal is one where everybody is happy. The best way to accomplish this is to be fair in all your dealings and to insist that others be fair with you. Remember this when negotiating the terms, conditions, costs, and fees of a public offering.

The process of taking a private company public is not an everyday business transaction, but it's one that is often the culmination of several years of success and growth. One hopes your company will reach the level of success where you will be considering such a step in the future. If so, this chapter will have helped to shed some light on the mysteries of going public.

When the time comes, use the information in this chapter. Examine your alternatives in an objective and professional manner before making your decisions. That way, whatever those decisions are, you can be sure they will be the right ones.

CHAPTER 8

ADVERTISING, PROMOTION, AND PUBLIC RELATIONS

Hard-hitting facts for better results

In This Chapter:

1. The terms defined and explained
    - Advertising
    - Promotion
    - Public Relations ("PR")
2. The ten commandments of advertising
    - I. Determine spending limits
    - II. Don't use radio or TV at first
    - III. Don't advertise in yearbooks or programs
    - IV. Create an image
    - V. Use direct mail
    - VI. Try the local paper
    - VII. Try regional editions of major newspapers
    - VIII. Generate publicity once a month
    - IX. Create "events" regularly
    - X. Monitor results closely
3. Direct mail: The most effective advertising

Much more can be said about advertising, promotion and public relations than we will cover in this chapter. This area of business is one of the most important, and the reader would be well-served to seek out a few books that are devoted entirely to the subject.

It is not the intention of this chapter to make experts out of our readers but rather to identify and explain certain selected methods and ideas. These proven techniques will bring excellent results, and some common mistakes made by even experienced businesspeople can be avoided.

What works and what doesn't? Sometimes only time will tell which methods are best. Experiment with various media and ideas. Try several approaches and carefully monitor the results. No better way exists to discover what works than to record your actual experience.

THE TERMS DEFINED AND EXPLAINED

Many businesspeople are confused about the differences between advertising, promotion, and public relations. They're not all just different words for the same thing. It's important that any overall marketing strategy include plans for each of them. So before we go any further, each of these areas will be addressed separately.

Advertising

An effective advertisement emphasizes the desirable qualities of a product or service. This directive sets advertising apart from public relations, which promotes a good public feeling toward a company in general. The desirable qualities that are emphasized might be "newer," "better," "faster," "less expensive," or other adjectives that offer something of benefit to the reader, listener, or viewer.

Recent marketing and psychological research suggests that there are several key words that are the most persuasive in the language, and these words should be included in your advertising to describe your product when applicable. These words are

save   *new*
discovery   *results*
health   *proven*
easy   *love*
money   *you*
guarantee   *free*

An important element of advertising is that it arouses a desire to buy or patronize. To be most effective, ads must contain what is referred to as a "call to action"—a message such as "Buy Now!" or "Call Today!" An advertiser's primary intention is *not* to create a good feeling in the mind of the buying public (although that *can* be a legitimate *secondary* goal). It is simply to motivate them to *buy* or *patronize*.

Promotion

Most people think of a promotion as an event to attract public interest. Examples of such events are the "tent sales" given by automobile dealers and such national affairs as the Publishers' Clearing House Sweepstakes. These events attract attention and, in doing so, frequently increase the sales of the products or services offered by the firm holding the event.

The most effective promotions are those that use an appealing event, supported by a coordinated advertising and publicity campaign. But the publicity generated by such an event should not be left to chance: Phone calls should be made to newspapers, radio stations, and television news desks. The news item should be briefly and carefully explained to the assignment editor. These phone calls can be preceded by a press release that explains the event in brief, clear prose.

When a promotion is planned, it is conventional to rely upon the press for some free coverage. Some people are a bit awkward or uneasy about this. They feel they're trying to get something for nothing. But don't be intimidated by the press. Remember that they must fill their newspapers, or their radio and television news shows, everyday, seven days a week.

If an event is put together that has legitimate mass appeal, and the information provided to the press is concise and well-written, then the media's job is made easier. This is one less story they'll have to produce. And don't worry if your story isn't accepted the first time: Keep trying.

Public Relations

Simply stated, public relations, or PR, is the art of creating a "nice guy" image for businesspeople and their companies.

People naturally prefer doing business with those they like, especially if it comes to choosing between two nearly identical companies. A standard definition of public relations speaks of rapport, goodwill, and neighborly interchange, and these are the key words that should act as a guide in creating a public relations program for every company.

Public relations will be improved when an event, or "promotion," is geared toward satisfying the customers and the marketplace. This can be accomplished by centering the event on something noncommercial, like professional athletes signing autographs for youngsters, or a benefit accruing to a charity or community cause. With well-planned advertising and publicity calling attention to the event, the resulting PR will be positive and long-lasting.

Good, positive PR is an important contributor to the long-range success of a business. Many smaller businesses ignore this means of entrenching their companies in the mind and heart of their market. PR can be used to great advantage if you take the time for it and do it correctly.

As a result of hands-on experience, we have developed what we call "The Ten Commandments of Advertising." These dos and don'ts are intended for those who are not experts in advertising. If these rules are followed, a business should see an improvement in its sales, its image, and its bottom line over a period of time.

THE TEN COMMANDMENTS OF ADVERTISING
(Most Appropriate for New Businesses)

I. Spending Limits

Some call it budgeting. A better definition might be "the smart way to keep from overspending." One of the easiest mistakes to make in any business is to spend too much on advertising—more than you can really afford. The spending gets away from the management if they don't use discipline.

So start with a firm promise to stick with the spending limit you establish. You may be tempted to modify the budget after only two or three months. Resist the temptation. Wait a while. Don't allow advertising salespeople to influence your decision on the budget. Remember, these people have one-track minds: They want to sell, sell, sell. That's how they make their living.

How much should be set aside for advertising? Many companies budget about 5 percent of expected sales for their advertising, promotion, and public relations expenses. Radio Shack budgets around 7 percent. Other companies spend only 3 percent of sales. It's all right to experiment a bit every few months. Start out with 5 percent of sales and see what kind of response you get. Then, in a few months, experiment with a little more or less, and see what happens. But stick with whatever amount was originally budgeted for a while, and don't experiment too often. It may take several months to really gauge the results.

II. Don't Use Radio or TV at First

There is nothing quite like seeing your own television commercial for the first time or hearing your first radio spot. Your pride takes great leaps, and your ego is stroked. But radio and television aren't the most effective means of advertising for a young business. This is especially true if the business has only a single location.

Unless the public already knows the business's location, or unless there are widely dispersed locations within the reach of the broadcast, a lot of money can be spent only to pad an owner's ego. That's bad business, and it's a waste of money.

Radio and television commercials cost a great deal to produce. Don't think the radio or television station's in-house production crew will do a quick and inexpensive ad for you that will be effective (although that's what you'll be told). The ad will wind up *looking* and *sounding* quick and inexpensive. It is always best to use a professional independent advertising agency.

Expect to spend at least $1000 to have a radio spot created and about $5000 for a television commercial. And these production costs are only initial costs. Pockets have to be deep enough to pay for an advertising campaign of several weeks' duration, with at least four or five spots airing each day during prime time.

The most effective radio and television campaigns are those supported by newspaper advertising and by concentrated efforts at publicity and promotion. The reason for this is that the best of radio and television commercials present only *one* product, *one* event, or *one* message during their 15- to 60-second duration. During this short time, potential customers will not learn location, information on other products or services, or prices. The only way to overcome this, especially for a new company with a product, service, or location the public hasn't seen before is to repeat the radio or TV spot many, many times. The cost of this would be crippling. So don't try radio or television until your company is well enough established that the public will recognize the company name and identify it with specific goods and services.

III. Don't Advertise in Yearbooks or Programs

Think of this type of advertising strictly as a donation. The positive effect on sales will be very minimal, if any at all. The only result will be that the salesperson will receive a commission and the organization printing the booklet or program will receive some money.

A new business will be besieged by countless solicitors trying to convince you to advertise in their special program. It's amazing to find there are so many of these organizations, all asking for money. Some of the causes are going to be worthy ones, and it will be hard at first to resist their pitch. But once you've learned that these requests are endless, and they won't increase sales one dollar, it will be easier to say no.

If you really like one of these organizations, it is probably better off if you simply give it a donation. But don't be deluded into thinking that anything spent on brochures or programs is going to help sell products or services. It won't.

Another comment you'll often hear from people selling advertising or soliciting contributions is, "It's deductible." Just remember that a profit must be made before *anything* can be deducted. Even then, dollars are still dollars. They can always be put into something that will help your business and *still* be deductible. Don't let these solicitors convince you that a dollar given to them is somehow a different dollar than could be used for some other purpose. If you give, give from the heart, with complete understanding of what you're doing.

IV. Create an Image

A professionally designed logo and a standard printed ad format are the first steps in creating a company's image. Everyone is familiar with the Chrysler pentastar, or the initials IBM, or McDonald's golden arches. We recognize these images, called *logos*, and automatically identify with the companies they represent. Pick up any national magazine and look at the advertising produced by the big, successful companies. Notice that they use the same ad format—the same type style and borders—and they include the same logo in every ad. They have an image, and that's what you want, too. What works for the big boys will work for every business, no matter what its size.

How do you create an image? The first thing is to create a logo. Try to do some rough sketches of your own ideas, then use a professional commercial artist to refine the sketches. Let the artist give input regarding what works best. Examine the artist's ideas, make suggestions if you wish, and decide which logo is the best symbol for your company. Tell the artist to provide you with *finished artwork* that is *camera-ready*. This logo can then be printed on stationery and business forms, business cards, and exterior signs and can be used in newspaper ads.

It would also add to your image if your print ads all used the same border (the border is the heavy line surrounding the ad itself). Look in the newspaper for examples. The artist will have access to many format and border samples.

You may also want to create a slogan to use in ads, letterheads, business cards, packaging, and maybe even buttons for employees to wear. One of the most famous slogans used by a major company is Avis' "We try harder." The best slogans are short and to the point.

V. Use Direct Mail

Direct mail is so important that there is a separate section devoted to it in this chapter (following the Ten Commandments of Advertising). Direct mail advertising can be the most effective way to attract customers. Frequently, it's the best use of the advertising dollar. It's one of the most commonly overlooked forms of advertising, and that's an additional advantage: Fewer competitors will be using it to advertise *their* products or services.

VI. Try the Local Paper

The key word here is *try*. Many times the community paper is a waste of money and simply doesn't pull in the customers. And for certain types of businesses, the local paper just doesn't make sense. Wholesalers, for example, should forget the local paper altogether. Their best advertising is going to be direct mail, followed up by telephone solicitation of those who received the mailing pieces.

For businesses in retail sales and service, newspaper ads *can* be the most effective advertising tool. The only way to find out is to try it and see what happens. If it works, good. If it doesn't, not too much will have been lost as long as the results have been carefully monitored (see Commandment #10). Be sure to follow the principles of good print advertising: Use a logo and a slogan, don't try to say too much, use a headline that will attract attention, and include a "call to action."

VII. Try Regional Editions of a Major Newspaper

If your business is located in a major metropolitan area, it will be a real shock to see the advertising rates for newspapers. Rates have more than doubled since 1977, and the major newspapers have priced themselves right out of the budget of most smaller advertisers. To counteract this development, which would have cost millions in lost revenue, the large daily papers have created editions that cover specific geographic segments of their market. In Detroit, for example, the major dailies have editions called North Metro, East Suburban, Downriver, North-west, and Metro. Each regional edition carries an advertising rate that is only a fraction of the rate for the entire circulation of the paper, the "full run." This allows the small businessperson to advertise in a selected area for a reasonable price. The ads reach only those readers who are most likely to patronize the business.

Some magazines also have regional editions, but it's best to stay away from magazine advertising until your business is well established.

VIII. Generate Publicity Once a Month

Remember, publicity is free advertising. Newspapers need to fill their pages day after day. If a well-drafted announcement, called a *press release*, offers the newspaper some newsworthy information, then it will prompt some free coverage.

The first concern is to find something that can truly be called newsworthy. A good source of ideas is the newspaper itself. Read the headlines in the local and business section every day. Look for *anything* that sparks a story idea that would appeal to the editors of that particular paper. Once you've come up with an idea, try to write a headline for it. Then write a brief press release, using the same style of writing as is used in other articles in the same newspaper. Type the press release neatly, double-spaced, with the words "PRESS RELEASE" and "For Immediate Release" at the top. Send it to the editor or to the attention of the department that would cover this topic, such as the business desk or the sports editor.

If the paper is interested in the story, they may phone for an interview, or they may simply edit your release and run it in the paper without notifying you. Keep an eye on the paper for mention of your company, but if they don't use your first submission, don't be discouraged. Try again next month. Don't make yourself a pest, but keep trying.

Use publicity as often as possible. It is more readily believed than paid advertising, and it helps to establish a company in the eyes of the public. Take advantage of this free and effective business tool.

IX. Create Events Regularly

We all see the inevitable Washington's Birthday Sale and Fourth of July Sale, as well as the car dealers with their tent sales. These are EVENTS. They give these businesses an excuse to do something to bring in customers, and bringing in customers is how sales are made.

You can stage an event by having one or two hometown sport stars appear at your place of business to meet youngsters and autograph footballs or baseballs or t-shirts. If your business doesn't deal with the general public, the sports stars can be brought in to meet your customers and their children at a special picnic.

There are many ideas that you can use: Just look at what others are doing in different businesses. If you see something appropriate for your business, give it a try. These events, or promotions, will be fun. They will encourage customers to think well of your business, and they will help build a business with a strong customer base.

An important part of every successful event is a coordinated effort at promoting the event through advertising and publicity. Everything must be properly organized to ensure its success. Make a list of deadlines, costs, and things to do well in advance of the date of the event. If you don't coordinate things, you'll feel pretty foolish when only a few people show up. You may not have a smashing success the first time you try a promotion. But you will have learned something if you critique the results.

X. Monitor Results Closely

One of the most valuable tools for the improvement and success of a business is a written log containing everything that's been done in advertising, publicity, and promotion, with comments on the effectiveness of each. You should be able to sit down and assess every ad run over the past year, every promotion, every direct mail campaign, and each press release. This will help determine what worked, what didn't, and why. From this, you can determine a pattern of success that will ensure better results in the future.

Apply These Rules

Apply these "Ten Commandments" and experiment—while staying within budget—until you've found what works best in your particular business, geographic area, and competitive environment. There are other choices: Experiment with no rules to guide you, or refrain from doing any advertising or promotion at all. The former will waste money with an uncoordinated and nonproductive advertising program; the latter will ignore a wide group of potential customers and by doing so will lose sales and profits. Be aggressive and work smart. Develop a plan that will produce results, and build your company's image, sales, and profits.

DIRECT MAIL: THE MOST EFFECTIVE ADVERTISING

One of the main problems with traditional advertising media like newspapers, television, and radio is that advertisers pay for a message to a general audience. The message, however, will be important only to a limited portion of that audience. In short, you're paying for a lot of useless coverage. Direct mail eliminates most of this useless coverage by targeting only specific groups.

Most businesses draw their customers from some specific group with distinctive characteristics and traits. A laundry and dry-cleaning service, for example, or a retail hardware store might expect the majority of its business to come from a geographic area measured in terms of driving time to the store. A wholesaler might draw its business from a certain type of retail store or from companies engaged in manufacturing specific items. These groups are called "customer bases."

Not all businesses have customer bases narrow enough to warrant using direct mail. Burger King, for example, sells to such a diverse group that *regular* advertising is actually more effective. But for those companies who do have well-defined customer bases, direct mail is an excellent means of advertising.

Mailing Lists

Compiling or buying the proper mailing list is an important first step. For wholesalers, or for any company working in a national market, mailing lists can be obtained from trade associations. These mailing lists can usually be broken down into categories by interest or region. Another source of names and addresses is through list brokers. These can usually be found in the Yellow Pages under "Advertising—Direct Mail." Simply look for firms whose ads mention mailing lists. Several large national mailing list companies can be found in advertisements in the monthly magazines of the advertising and marketing industry.

If your market is small enough, you might even be able to produce your own mailing list. Use directories found at the local public library, such as Standard & Poor's *Directory of Corporations*. For local businesses, use a publication called *Bresser's Directory* (or one similar to it). This directory lists the name and mailing address of almost everyone in the city by geographic area and street address.

Once a mailing list has been compiled, it's imperative to come up with an effective way to deliver the message. Direct mail is expensive. The secret of success with direct mail advertising rests on these two elements:

1. Succeeding in getting the recipient of the mail to actually *open the envelope* and read what's inside.
2. Putting the *right* message inside the envelope.

The Envelope

Junk mail arrives by the sackful in everyone's mailbox, and it's almost always easy to identify: colorful envelopes covered with messages, prize notifications, folders and catalogs, and many other variations on the same principles. Most of us treat this junk mail with the respect it deserves: We throw it away unopened.

Consider the mail you *don't* automatically toss in the trash. What does it look like? The envelope probably looks like a "real" envelope, perhaps bearing a tasteful logo along with the return address. But most significantly, it is not addressed to "Occupant." Your name and address have been typed on the envelope, not on a stick-on mailing label. This personalized envelope is one you would be likely to open yourself. It's also the type to mail to those on your mailing list.

The Message

Now for what goes *inside* the envelope: a sheet of genuine stationery, with the company's logo on the letterhead, addressed personally to the recipient as would befit any normal business correspondence. The letter should have a personal salutation, such as "Dear Mr. Jones" instead of "Dear Sir." It should begin with a one-sentence first paragraph like

> I'm writing this letter to tell you about an easy, new approach to buying home electronics, an approach that's *guaranteed* to save you money.

This first sentence needs to be a real grabber. It's a good place to use as many of those "12 most persuasive words" mentioned earlier as will fit. The objective, of course, is to catch the reader's attention so he'll read on.

The body of the letter should contain one *brief* paragraph explaining the offer and another shorter paragraph to reinforce the offer. Reinforcement is accomplished through statements like the following:

> We take pride in our service, and we guarantee it's the quickest and most courteous in the industry. Nothing is more important to us than the satisfaction of you, the customer.

The letter should end with a "call to action." Ask the customer to *do something*, whether it's to

> Call me personally at 555-3322 for a special introductory discount

or

> Come by our showroom for a personal demonstration.

Making a special offer that will expire soon gives the customer an additional incentive to act, and act immediately.

An Alternative to In-house Direct Mail

If a business does not have the personnel or equipment to process personalized letters, search for a secretarial service that handles direct mail. They will enter the names and addresses from the mailing list you choose into their word processor or computer. Using stationery provided by the advertiser, their computer will print an individually addressed letter, with personalized salutation, to every name on the list. Each letter looks like an original, and it is! Envelopes will be addressed automatically. All the advertiser does is sign, seal, and stamp each letter. Most secretarial firms charge for this service on an hourly basis. The cost is generally between $100 and $150 for 200 letters. This cost, of course, doesn't include stationery, envelopes, postage, and the cost of the mailing lists.

Direct mail is not inexpensive. But if the right formula is found and it generates a good response, direct mail can be a genuine bargain. Start small, and experiment with 50 to 100 pieces in "test mailings." Then monitor the results. Then, when you find the combination that works, increase the size of the mailing.

This approach to direct mail will bring you the highest amount of customer dollars for every advertising dollar spent. And one thing of which you can be certain: Your competition *won't* be doing it.

In Summary

This chapter was written for those who are faced with making daily decisions regarding advertising, promotion, and public relations. There are many books on the subject that go into far more detail than is available here, and we recommend that the practicing entrepreneur read a few of these.

Our intention here has been only to lay a groundwork for you to build on: our Ten Commandments. But by following the strategies we've summed up for you in this chapter, and by tailoring your methods after monitoring the results, you should find your sales and profits growing at a healthy rate.

CHAPTER 9

HIRING ATTORNEYS
AND ACCOUNTANTS

The professional way to hire professionals

In This Chapter:

1. The right professionals for you
2. Finding the right specialist
3. The selection process
4. Interviewing the professionals
5. A guide to billings and rates
6. Negotiating fees

THE RIGHT PROFESSIONALS FOR YOU

Hiring the right professional can be an important advantage to a business, especially if that business is a startup. Conversely, hiring the wrong ones can do irreparable harm. You should hire your attorney and accountant as carefully as you would hire a key employee, because the right professional will be an asset in raising capital, structuring the ownership and control of your business, and establishing important business contacts.

The information and assistance that these attorneys and accountants can offer goes well beyond what would normally be considered their areas of expertise.

FINDING THE RIGHT SPECIALIST

Most professionals, whether they are medical doctors, engineers, or attorneys and accountants, are specialists. When you hire an attorney to act as your corporate counsel and adviser, you don't want to choose one who is a generalist, claiming expertise in criminal law, divorce law, estates, and every other law specialty. Don't educate an attorney in corporate or securities law at your expense! Hire one who is already experienced and competent in the business specialties, not just one who *says* she is.

And in hiring an accountant, you want to find one with most of the learning curve behind him, one with experience in the industry you are entering. This way, you are assured your advisers have seen most of the mistakes made by companies in your industry, and they can help you avoid the same mistakes. They will also be able to advise you of the things that the successful companies in your field have done in order to create their success.

This way, you benefit from years of experience and thousands of dollars of past learning experiences (otherwise known as *mistakes*) that other companies have been through. The inexperienced attorney or accountant can be a real hindrance to you. They'll be learning right along with you, and the ones who will benefit the most are their future clients. Think of it this way: Would you want to be the first patient in a neurosurgeon's career? Somebody has to be, but it shouldn't be you!

THE SELECTION PROCESS

Find Out Who Is Available

Both attorneys and accountants are listed in the Yellow Pages under general headings as well as under various specialties. Just because a professional is listed under a particular specialty, however, doesn't necessarily mean that he or she has any more experience in that area than the average practitioner.

You'll see what we mean when you look in your Yellow Pages and find the same attorney's name under several, or even *all*, of the specialty areas of the law. Can this attorney possibly be a specialist in all these areas? Obviously not.

Although the Yellow Pages can be a good starting point in gathering names, don't rely on the accuracy of the listings alone. Do some more digging. Again, compare the hiring process to that which you would go through to hire a key employee. Would you rely exclusively on the resume you had been given, or would you ask questions of the job applicant and check her references?

An excellent source of information on attorneys is the Martindale-Hubbell Law Directory that can be found in almost every library. This directory lists members of the Bar Association by geographical location, by firm, and by specialty. Consulting such a directory allows you to find information on the education, age, and special training of local attorneys. Your reference librarian can help you find the directory should you have trouble locating it in the library.

INTERVIEWING THE PROFESSIONALS

Continue your selection process until you have come up with at least three candidates, then call each of the firms. If your references are for a firm and not for any particular individual, then ask to speak to someone regarding "retaining your firm for legal (or accounting) work." You may be asked for a brief description of the type of business you're in, so someone can match you with the specialist most suited to your needs.

When you reach that person, tell her, "I am setting up (or acquiring) a new business and am interviewing law (or accounting) firms before I select one to do our work. Your firm is one of the three I've chosen to interview." You might want to give your source or referring person or other reference at this point. Then ask, "What is the procedure for arranging an interview *at your offices*, preferably next week?"

The person you've reached will most likely ask you about

your business and plans, trying to size you up. In case someone should ask, we suggest you *not* reveal the other firms you're considering *before* making your selection.

Conduct the Interviews

When it comes time for the interview, arrive dressed in a business suit and be on time. You should expect this same promptness from the professional, and this may help you judge whether she really has the time for you. When you enter the meeting room and get settled, *you* be the first to speak. Take control of the situation. You're doing the hiring.

Reiterate the purpose of the interview—that you want to learn what this individual and her firm can offer you and your company. Mention that her firm is one of three firms you are interviewing and that you expect to make a decision within seven days. Explain briefly the type of business you are starting or acquiring and what you think your most immediate and obvious needs might be (such as raising capital or establishing an accounting system). Then, let the attorney or accountant talk.

Listen carefully to what she has to say. Take notes. Try to judge whether her personality is compatible with yours. Is she aggressive enough? Does she seem honestly interested in your project? After she has finished speaking, consider whether she has addressed the following questions, and if not, ask her to do so.

Considerations in the Selection Process

• Similar clients. Does she have any other clients in a noncompeting line of business that is similar to yours? If so, you may find her better able to anticipate your business's problems and needs.
• Competing clients. Does she have any clients in the *same* industry as you? If so, how would she handle a conflict of interest, should one arise? If she doesn't, would she accept a competing client who came to the firm *after* you?
• Who does the work? Who would be the partner-in-charge of your account? To whom would you speak on a day-to-day basis

about your account? (Often, especially in larger firms, the senior partner-in-charge, with whom you're speaking, may turn the account over to a junior partner who supervises even lower-level staff people doing the actual work. This may make the partner further removed from the account than you would like.)

• Billing rates. What are the billing rates (hourly charges) for each person who will work with you?

• How must you pay? What special provisions are made for the billings and retainers of new accounts?

• What are the recurring fees? Is there a flat-rate fee for things like incorporations and annual minutes (for attorneys), or for year-end tax work and monthly financial statement preparation (for accountants)?

• Maximum fees. Will she quote a "cap"—a maximum fee—for services requiring hourly billing?

• Method of billing. How frequent are the billings, and how detailed will they be? (If five staff members provided different services during the month, would you be able to tell which staff level performed which service, or would the bill simply state "services rendered . . . . $850.00"?)

• Who is ultimately responsible for billings? With whom would you speak if there were questions about a bill?

Concluding the Interview

After covering these last items, ask if there is anything else you should know about the firm. Then thank the individual for arranging the interview and tell her you will be making a decision within a week.

A GUIDE TO BILLINGS AND RATES

Professional fees can quickly grow to a staggering size if you don't try to control them, but controlling them is difficult if you don't understand how the professionals bill for their time in the first place. Because attorneys and accountants are significantly different in the way they bill, we'll explore them separately.

Billing and Rates for Attorneys

Attorney fees currently range from $75 per hour to $200 per hour and more. However, not all legal work is billed on an hourly basis, and not all of it is actually performed by an attorney.

Who Does the Work?

If you were to call your attorney and ask to have a commercial lease drafted for your business, your attorney would probably ask his or her secretary to run a copy of a similar lease off the word processor. That copy might go to a law clerk (usually a law student in training) or a paralegal aide who would make most or all of the necessary changes to personalize the lease for your business and circumstances. Finally, the lease would return to your attorney for a final review.

In total, there may have been several hours involved in generating this lease, but those hours are not all partner hours to be billed at $75 to $200. Most of the time was provided by the paralegal and the secretary, and that's why it's important to ask about the billing rates of *all* people who might be working on your account. Depending on the size of the law firm you choose, the number of people who may work on your account can vary quite a lot.

Flat Rates

Just as this lease agreement was produced with relative ease by your attorney, so can a great number of business agreements and forms be produced by your attorney by simply making minor modifications to a standard form or one used previously.

In fact, this is similar to the way most attorneys set up corporations: They take a standard incorporation package, add the name of your company and its authorized number of shares, modify one or two clauses (if you want something slightly out of the ordinary), and generate this package from a word processor or a memory typewriter.

This is why you should inquire about "flat rates" for new incorporations, annual minutes, and other fairly standardized services. Most law firms will charge a fixed fee for these—

simple incorporations generally range from $250 to $600—and you should be able to get a quote in advance. Because so many of the services you may need from your attorney are produced in a similar manner, it's probably wise to ask for a cap on any service she performs. And always remember that you have every right to negotiate fees.

Billing and Rates for Accountants

The hourly rate for accountants can run anywhere from $35 to $175 and up, but just as with attorneys, not all the time you will be billed for will be that of an accountant.

There are four primary services provided by most full service accounting firms: tax work, standard accounting services (preparation of financial statements and reports), auditing, and "management advisory services" (assisting with the organizational operations within a company).

Accounting and Financial Statement Preparation
Standard accounting services can range from the preparation of the forecasted financial statements (projections) you need to raise your initial capital, to the production of monthly or quarterly financial statements for your management's use, to annual financial statements you might show to your outside investors.

The amount of partner time involved in these statements, and hence their expense, depends to a large extent on the size of your company and the amount of work your employees do to get the information ready for the accountants.

Periodic Billing Rates
Many companies don't feel they have the resources or the need to have a full-time accountant on their staff. Instead, they might hire a part-time bookkeeper to pay bills and keep their bank accounts balanced, or the owner or manager might even perform this function personally. Then, once a month, all the check stubs, bank statements, and sales journals are brought to an accounting firm, which produces a set of financial statements for the business.

This type of service can almost always be arranged at a set monthly fee ranging from around $200 per month to $500 or more, depending on the size of the accounting firm and the size of your company. If it costs more than this for monthly financial statements to be prepared, then you're nearly always justified in hiring a staff accountant.

Annual Accounting and Tax Services

If you don't want or need monthly or quarterly financial statements, then you may want to negotiate to have your annual financial statements prepared in a package deal along with your annual income tax returns. The vast majority of the work that must be performed to produce annual financial statements has to be done to prepare the tax returns anyway, so it shouldn't cost very much more to get a set of financial statements prepared when the year-end tax work is done.

For a very small company, annual tax returns may cost only a few hundred dollars. But because they can run into thousands of dollars for larger companies, especially if no other accounting work has been performed during the year, it's in your best interest to request that a cap be set on the fee.

Auditing Services

Auditing is a special service provided only by Certified Public Accountants (CPAs). No other accountant is legally able to provide it. The CPA analyzes the books and records of the company, reviews its controls over cash, inventory, and other assets, and seeks confirmation of its liabilities. After this work is completed, the CPA firm attaches a letter to the financial statements either endorsing the statements as being substantially accurate or enumerating problems uncovered during the audit. Audit fees range from a few thousand dollars to tens of thousands, and a fee should always be agreed on in advance.

Other Accounting Services

Other accounting services include general management help, employee payroll reporting, and visits to bank loan officers or potential investors. If you have chosen a quality professional from a good firm, much more will be available than just tax preparation and what is normally thought of as "accounting" services. The fees for these other services should be negotiated in advance, if possible.

NEGOTIATING FEES

Remember that *you* are hiring these professionals, and that puts you in the driver's seat. It's your right and responsibility to negotiate and question bills you receive. Whenever you know you are requesting a professional service that can be costly, be certain you also establish how and at what rate you will be billed for this service.

If travel is involved, determine if airfare will be first class or coach, if meals will be covered by a per diem allowance, and at what rate travel time will be charged (travel time can *almost always* be negotiated to a reduced rate). Always try to have either a fixed rate negotiated for the services or a cap to limit the fee. Lacking this, at least request to have interim bills sent to you so you can monitor the cost of the services and avoid any unpleasant surprises. (And there can be some big surprises!)

The Final Analysis

Even though cost is an important consideration when choosing a professional to work with, it shouldn't be your *only* consideration. When you are raising capital, financial statements prepared by a prestigious accounting firm may result in a better perception of you and your company by investors. Likewise, a legal opinion supplied by a well-known law firm could mean the difference between success and failure in an offering.

Also, remember that attorneys and accountants deal daily with dozens of monied and influential members of the business and investment community, and their professional contacts can be valuable to you in many ways. They may turn out to be the best salespeople for your money needs, bringing potential investors to your company.

In addition, it is critically important that *you* be able to work closely with the professional and trust his or her judgment. Be sure there will be no personality conflict between you. Ideally, your relationship will be a long-lived one.

Finally, if you hire one of these professionals and find you are not happy with her, tell her so. Don't feel uncomfortable about your relationship or wonder whether *you're* the one who's really at fault.

If you remain unhappy, *fire* the individual. *You* are the boss, and you should be pleased with her work and how she conducts herself. Don't concern yourself too much over who is to blame for the problems.

On the other hand, if you *are* pleased, tell her that, too. A sincere compliment can go a long way in cementing a relationship with a top-notch professional. And having a top-notch professional on your team can help you immeasurably as you strive to achieve your business goals.

CHAPTER 10

MANAGING A BUSINESS
FOR MAXIMUM PROFIT

Putting time and people to work for you

In This Chapter:

1. Using a management team
2. Choosing a board of directors
3. Employees as a management resource
4. Credos of good employee management
5. Employee incentive programs
6. Management of executive time
7. Combining management with goals

Management as a Field of Study

Management is certainly a popular topic today. Detailed studies of management techniques have been published by many experts, and thousands of books and articles on the topic seem to appear each year. Courses on the "science" of management are presented regularly at universities and business schools across the country.

Some of this academic focus has resulted in the branding of management as little more than useless theories and formulas dreamed up by out-of-touch professors. This view is especially popular with many of today's self-made managers and entrepreneurs who feel that managing a business is something properly learned by *doing* rather than by studying.

It is true that academic courses on management can't really

teach someone to *be* a good manager. What the better courses teach are merely the philosophies and styles that other managers have found successful. But each company is different, and each manager's personality is unique, so what is best will vary greatly from situation to situation.

Bluntly put, you can study management until you retire, and you *still* may not learn the secret of good management.

Management philosophies, styles, and techniques, however, should still be important to anyone who is engaged in the daily operation of a business. Nearly every decision a businessperson makes is important to the success of that business. The first step toward making the right decisions is to be aware of the importance of those decisions. Each decision should be analyzed closely to find the best and most profitable solution. If you don't find the best and most profitable solution, some competitor *will*.

USING A MANAGEMENT TEAM

One of the first things to learn is that all the best business strategies are immediately apparent to no one individual. Sometimes it takes the insight of someone who deals with customers on a one-to-one basis to see what is needed. Other times it might take the skill and experience of an outside professional. Still other times, it might require someone removed from the daily operations but with an ongoing interest in a company.

The first of these groups—the people who deal with customers on a day-to-day basis—consists of your employees. Their role in a company's quest for success will be discussed later in this chapter. The second group—outside professionals—have already been discussed in Chapter 9. The last group—people with an ongoing interest in your company but who are removed from the daily operations—is dominated by the board of directors.

CHOOSING A BOARD OF DIRECTORS

In a large company, especially one owned by public shareholders, the duty of a board of directors is to monitor the managers of the company. If those managers don't properly serve the interests of the shareholders, the board removes them. In a smaller, privately held company, though, a board's purpose is to offer a broad scope of experienced opinions to the managers of the company, who are usually the owners as well. To summarize:

Big Public Company Board's job: keep an eye on management.
Private Company Board's job: offer advice and counsel.

The first response of most private business owners is "Why should I have to tell a bunch of outsiders what I am doing in my business?" There are many good reasons for having a board, but one of the most important is that everyone, including owners and experienced managers, is fallible. Having a truly objective viewpoint on which way to do things is often indispensable. The idea is to surround yourself with people who are at least as smart as you and who have more or different experience.

To hire these people as full-time employees would be prohibitively expensive and probably impossible. But a company can get the benefit of their experience and training by offering them the hallowed and prestigious role of director of the company. A million dollars' worth of brains can be had for a bargain basement price in this manner. But it's important to know whom to approach and how to approach them.

Whom to Approach for a Position on the Board

Don't ask a family physician or dentist to sit on the board. He or she is probably excellent at medical or dental care but will most likely make a poor business adviser. Contrary to some opinions, having doctors and dentists on a company's board of directors does not give prestige to the board. The contrary is actually true, as bankers and businesspeople know that doctors and dentists are among those with the worst track records in business dealings, particularly in operating businesses. They may do well as income earners or as passive investors, but as businesspeople they rank very low on the totem pole.

Attributes of Good Board Members

The people who should be targeted as board members for a company should have the following qualities:

1. They must be *experienced*. The more years they have spent in business, the better.
2. Their skills and expertise should *complement* the existing management's. There's no sense in having two bottle washers and no cooks.
3. They should be *respected* in the business community. The community's regard for board members can open many doors otherwise closed to the business.
4. They must be willing to *commit* to at least a one-year term.

An ideal board for a business run by an entrepreneur who is very proficient in manufacturing might be made up of the following: (1) a member who has 25 years' experience in sales as a manufacturer's representative, (2) a banker who has specialized in commercial lending for 15 years, (3) a successful entrepreneur who has taken a startup and built it into a profitable public company, (4) a CPA who is a senior partner with a large regional or national firm, and who has been professionally involved with manufacturing companies, (5) the business owner himself, and (6) either the major investor or the key employee of the company.

This board of directors could supply valuable advice and information to the fledgling entrepreneur in key areas: selling and marketing, financing and bank borrowing, building a company and taking it public. Together they would provide an excellent view of the company from a perspective other than the owner's or entrepreneur's.

How to Compensate Board Members

It's imperative that the members of a board of directors realize they are becoming part of a serious, businesslike undertaking. The best way to bring them to this realization is to conduct formal board meetings on a regular basis (at least every six months, but preferably quarterly or bimonthly) and to *pay* them for attending these meetings.

If top people have been selected, they are probably earning six-figure annual incomes in their own right, and they must be compensated at a fair rate. Major companies pay their directors as much as $5,000 or $10,000 for each meeting they attend, but a small company doesn't have to match this figure. A director's fee of $100 per meeting should be sufficient compensation.

Many directors of smaller companies accept their directorships because they feel flattered to be asked, and many enjoy the challenge of helping a growing firm through the exciting early stages of growth. Of course, your directors may be more excited if they are offered an option to purchase some shares in your company. That way, if the company they are helping is successful and winds up making a lot of money or going public, the directors will also benefit from the success and the role they played in it. This prospect for further personal benefits can be quite an incentive.

Board of Directors' Insurance

Some businesspeople will be reluctant to sit on a board of directors if they are are not covered by sufficient directors' liability insurance. Unfortunately, this is a bigger problem than it used to be, as reasonably priced directors' insurance is becoming more difficult to find. And more and more board members are being sued for any of a number of reasons relating to the businesses they oversee. It is certainly a good idea to have this type of insurance if it's available. Speak to an insurance agent who specializes in business insurance and ask about current costs and coverages.

The Corporate Attorney Can Help with Board Selection

If a company has selected an experienced corporate law specialist to act as its company counsel, the attorney should be able to explain the procedures for establishing a board of directors. Ask for an explanation of the terms that directors can serve and the effect of these terms. The attorney may agree to serve as Corporate Secretary or Assistant Secretary for purposes of the board meetings, but this could be an expensive way to record proceedings if she charges her normal hourly rates to do so.

With the right combination of people serving on your board of directors, your business can gain a sizable advantage over its competitors. The advice you receive will be invaluable, and the mere act of attending regular periodic board meetings will help focus your management's attention on long-range strategies that might otherwise be overlooked. The board of directors is a management tool that no good business should be without.

EMPLOYEES AS A MANAGEMENT RESOURCE

There is another resource that nearly all businesses possess yet which many of them do not use to its full potential: That resource is the business's own employees.

How to Motivate Employees

Most entrepreneurs and managers have little problem with self-motivation. The same goals that led them to start a business or to move up the ranks of an organization seem to motivate them to carry out their daily duties with enthusiasm. If anything, they are usually classic over-achievers.

But the lower-level employees of a company don't usually share that enthusiasm. What is *their* motivation for performing as well as they can?

The answer most often given is money—their salary—and this is a pretty good answer. After all, it's the reason the employee is at the job in the first place. But to think that money is the sole motivator of an employee is a big mistake, although it's a mistake made by 90 percent of the small businesses in existence today. To believe that money is the sole motivator is to sell short all the complexities of goals, aspirations, and desires that make people the individuals they are.

Most people want something more out of their job than just a paycheck. They would like to be an integral part of the whole business, not just a disposable unit. They would also like some recognition when they have performed their job better than average. *Never* underestimate the power of a pat on the back or the importance of being made to feel an important member of the team.

CREDOS OF GOOD EMPLOYEE MANAGEMENT

Here are some credos of good employee management:

Give credit where credit is due. This is especially important to those who have never been a "boss" before. *Never* usurp an employee's ideas or accomplishments and hold them out as your own. Nothing will stop the flow of ideas from employees quicker than not giving them credit for their own accomplishments. In fact, if there is any way to gracefully transfer the credit for an idea or accomplishment *to* an employee, you should do so even if most of the work or the concept came from *you*. Remember, you have nothing to prove to your employees.

Always be the last to give your opinion. Because employees are on the front line of a business—the ones who deal directly with customers and suppliers—they usually have valid ideas on better ways to service customers or economize operations. A sure way to *kill* the real opinions of your employees is to ask what they think of an idea, and then, before they respond, to tell them what *you* think of it. Even the best employee with the keenest insight into a problem is going to keep his or her opinion quiet and defer to the boss's opinion. Never fish for confirmation of your own ideas.

Let them know why. Nothing can demoralize employees more than having some new step added to their work—some extra duty they must perform—without their understanding of what it is they are doing and why it's necessary. Of course, management can always take the attitude that, "It needs to be done, and *that's* the reason." But employees resent that attitude, and their performance will show the resentment. Instead, tell the employees what you are trying to accomplish, and they'll wind up *helping* to accomplish it.

Get employees interested and involved. Employees can be one of the greatest assets of a company if they are convinced that they are an important part of your business and that the well-being of the business is as much their concern as management's. Make them feel like they're a part of the whole operation, not just a tiny cog in a big machine. Employees usually exercise the level of responsibility they are given; conversely, they'll seldom do anything more than is expected of them.

In the last few years, a few large national companies that had been experiencing constant product quality problems have implemented the seemingly radical idea of abolishing their separate Quality Control Department entirely. Amazingly, the level of their products' quality increased dramatically after this change. It seems that *all* the employees began to feel a responsibility for the quality of the products produced, and they did a better job of making them as a result.

Don't overcompartmentalize the staff. This credo is really an extension of the previous two rules: Let the employees know why, and keep them involved. Too often, in an attempt to organize the day-to-day operations of a business, a manager will try to allocate responsibility for every little task to a particular person. The rationale for this is understandable, but the results are often less than what the manager expected: Employees resent intrusion into their daily lives and resent the implication that they can't take responsibility for organizing these things themselves.

Suggest that *they* organize things among them, and let them *try* to work them out. Be there to help them if they need it, and they may if their personalities conflict. But whether they are successful at organizing their duties or they have some problems that management must solve for them, they'll appreciate the attitude of respect for their abilities, and they'll give more of their abilities in return.

Notice their accomplishments and compliment them. Nothing makes people work harder than knowing that what they do is appreciated. Some managers have the foolish belief that noting an employee's good work will only result in the employee's desire for an increase in pay. The two factors are surprisingly unrelated. But which would you prefer to have working for you, anyway: an underpaid but uninspired employee or one being paid a bit more but giving 110 percent?

Applying these credos of good employee management will result in an increase in productivity and better relations between a company and its customers and suppliers. Well-adjusted employees will be more accommodating with customers and much more concerned with the ultimate success of the business. And this gives the business another advantage over its competition.

Motivating Efficiently with Money

Naturally, it takes more than just good management credos to get employees to work. It also takes money! And money can be used to motivate employees in a number of creative ways. The amount of pay an employee receives can be more than just purchasing power. It can also be a means of keeping score of an employee's short-term contributions to the success of a business. Bonus pay programs can be established for modest amounts of cash that will motivate employees to perform at their best.

EMPLOYEE INCENTIVE PROGRAMS

Employee incentive programs are an important and vital tool for modern business. One indication of just *how* important they are comes from a recent poll by the accounting and management firm of Peat Marwick Main & Company. Not only did the poll show that 28 of the 100 fastest growing companies in America had such plans but, more importantly, *none* of the 100 *slowest* growing companies had one.

Sales managers have understood the motivational value of bonuses and commissions for years, but those same tools have been slow in crossing over from the sales floor to the rest of the company. Finally, though, that transition is taking place, and a number of companies have pioneered incentive programs for general staff and employees.

Let All Employees Participate

One of the first requirements of a good employee incentive plan is that the incentives take place throughout the entire company. If there are factory personnel or sales staff who are receiving bonuses because of increases in company sales or profits, then the general office staff and customer service people should be able to participate as well. Without this company-wide partici-pation, a feeling of resentment can develop that can lead to lack of cooperation among departments.

There are two ways to implement effective company-wide incentives.

1. Key the Incentives to Goals and Objectives the Employee Can Control

If one of the responsibilities of a company's bookkeeping department is making sure the accounts payable are paid in time to collect discounts from vendors, then offer a bonus each month if every available discount is taken. If the company has a customer service department, then conduct monthly customer satisfaction surveys and arrange bonuses for the department's employees based on the level of satisfaction shown in the surveys. Establish production levels for factory personnel to meet, with bonuses for each level they achieve.

The key factor is to be sure the employee actually has control over whatever it is that triggers the bonus.

After you develop a plan for each of the departments in a company, it's important to *promote the plan* to get all the benefits out of it that are possible. Borrow an idea from the salespeople and design a scoreboard on which the department personnel can keep track of their progress toward that month's goal. One of the biggest advantages of this type of plan is that it encourages all the employees in a department to work together to achieve a goal. Employees become aware that not only their own bonuses, but also those of all their fellow employees depend upon their work performance.

Don't feel that these bonuses have to be huge to have an effect. Even an extra $25 per month for each employee can provide motivation.

2. Create Company-wide Profitability Goals

Some companies have met with success by setting company-wide performance goals and establishing a pre-determined bonus for each department's employees. The plans are usually simple enough: The department decides on a targeted level of monthly or quarterly profit, and depending on whether that target is reached or by how much it is surpassed, a predetermined bonus is divided by each of the employees in the company.

In order for this program to work, management must be able to project what profits it thinks the company should make over the next year so it can set realistic and achievable goals. It often pays to keep things as simple as possible so the employees can fully understand how the system works.

A simple solution is to establish three separate targets: a "good," "better," and "best." The first of these levels (the good) might be company-wide profits of $100,000 for the quarter, the second (the better) would be $150,000, and the third (the best) would be $200,000 for the quarter. For each of these three levels, there is an established bonus for each employee, perhaps based on the employee's salary range.

For example, all employees earning up to $5.99 per hour would receive a bonus of $50 for helping achieve the "good" target, $75 for achieving the "better" one, and $125 for the "best" profit level of $200,000 per quarter. Those employees earning between $6 and $9.99 per hour would receive $75 for helping achieve the good target of $100,000, $100 for the better one, and $150 for the best profit level. Finally, employees earning anything over $10 per hour would receive $125, $150, or $200, depending on which of the three profit levels is reached.

Let Employees Constantly Monitor
Their Progress

Remember that one of the principal objectives of a bonus plan such as this is to give the employee the feeling that he or she is more than just a cog in a big machine. The goal is to get the message to them that management thinks they are an important part of the company—that the best interests of the company are *their* best interests as well. To get the most out of a plan such as this, employees should be kept constantly aware of their progress toward the monthly or quarterly goal.

Solicit employees' suggestions on improvements that could raise the company's overall profitability. (Suggestion boxes work much better when the employees realize they can actually profit from their own ideas.) And when the company *reaches* its goals (which it should do, unless those goals were set too high), *play up* the bonuses the employees have earned.

Promote the Company's Payment of Bonuses

Pick a Friday afternoon for a Bonus Day and gather your entire staff together (or groups of them, depending on your company's size) to pass out the bonus checks along with personal congratulations. Make a brief speech, maybe have refreshments served, and then let the staff off an hour early as an extra bonus. The amount of goodwill you can generate in this manner is incredible, and the cost is often no more than the equivalent to an extra day or two's pay.

Other Motivational Ideas

Profits don't have to be the only target for a bonus plan, of course. Sales, cost reductions, customer satisfaction, and quality improvement can all be used as targets if you can establish a consistent and fair way to measure them. Any plan will have to be customized to fit the peculiarities of a particular business. In fact, the entire system of employee benefits and bonuses *should* be customized for each unique situation. It's nearly impossible to lift a plan in its entirety from one company and expect it to be the most effective plan somewhere else.

Other interesting motivational ideas include individual bonuses for exemplary work, special bonuses to non-sales employees who generate a productive sales lead (called "lead commissions"), and bonuses for cost-cutting or quality-improving suggestions that the company implements.

Be Certain the Plan Will Work

The only word of warning we offer is this: It is *very* difficult to remove a bonus plan once it's been established. To do so causes a great deal of resentment on the part of the employees. So be as sure as possible that the plans installed are the best that can be produced. Before implementation, discuss the plans with the senior employees in each department to get their input and ideas.

But don't let caution stand in the way of establishing *some* means of rewarding employees for having achieved their goals. The very best way to keep customers happy is to be sure the employees who deal directly with them and who produce the product or service sold to them *want* to keep them happy. And the best way to do that is to make employees feel that they are a part of the team and that they will personally profit by pleasing the customer.

Cost Cutting and Higher Sales Aren't the Only Goals

Use caution when setting goals to be sure that so much emphasis isn't placed on cost cutting or sales levels that employees lose sight of the importance of customer satisfaction. Every staff meeting should include a reminder to employees that it is the customer who ultimately pays everyone's salary.

MANAGEMENT OF EXECUTIVE TIME

The topic of time management is one that is of a more personal nature than employee management and incentives. It is also an area that seems to plague many entrepreneurs and small business owners. They spend far too much of their time putting out fires when they should be directing their businesses at a higher level, analyzing the strategies they are using, and modifying them to bring in greater sales and more profits.

Spend Management Time on Important Issues

If a businessperson or manager falls into the common trap of reacting to daily situations rather than spending time on more important management activities, then each day will end in the same place it began. An effective manager isn't going to worry about minor day-to-day details but will delegate responsibility for those details to an employee.

Executives should spend time on improving morale, profit, and sales, or on upgrading the quality of products and services, or on a plan for business expansion. Time spent motivating employees is always well spent. Time spent doing things that other employees are paid to do, however, is time poorly spent. It is bad management.

A Personal Commitment Is Necessary

The management of time is difficult to teach because it requires a change in behavior on a consistent basis: Every hour of every day, a manager must be aware of the interruptions that can rob him of time. It's never any one interruption by itself that takes up the whole day, but a series of little ones. Each interruption seems harmless and short, and it's easy to give in to them when they arise.

Use an Effective Tool

A good manager will discipline himself to resist these interruptions. And there is a tool that can be invaluable in helping with this discipline: a daily appointment book. The concept sounds so simple that it's easy to dismiss as something you can do without. But you can't. This one simple tool can change the whole way a business is run.

We recommend the use of a pocket-sized daily appointment book, one designed for daily task-planning and scheduling. A book with one or two pages allotted for each weekday and a couple of lines for each hour of the day should work well.

Everything Must Be Scheduled

Then there must be a commitment to *use* the planner *every day* and *every hour* of every day *without fail*. The book should be carried everywhere, with everything scheduled *in advance* that needs to be accomplished each day. Each morning, at the beginning of the workday, check your daily schedule. Anything that *can* be delegated *should* be delegated.

This schedule will force you to spend less time on distractions and interruptions—the fires that can waste a businessperson's time—and allow you to spend more time on the important things. A genuine feeling of accomplishment will come at the end of each day when you scratch everything you've accomplished off the list. By improving your personal use of time, your ability to deal with the operation of a business will be greatly enhanced.

COMBINING MANAGEMENT WITH GOALS

Use the incentive programs we've described to motivate employees to put forth their very best effort. Keep them feeling like happy members of the team by practicing the credos of good management.

Take advantage of the advice of an experienced group of professionals by putting together a good board of directors to complement the knowledge and experience of your management team.

Be sure that the management team manages its own time well.

And be sure to spend sufficient time developing a long-term strategy so that you will always know the direction you want your business to take. Put *time* and *people* to work for your company, and it will be on its way to having truly effective management and the success and rewards that effective management brings.

APPENDIX A

THE "BIG EIGHT" ACCOUNTING FIRMS

The following is a list of accounting and auditing firms that have traditionally been regarded as the largest in the world.

During the past several years, a number of large firms have merged to create new giants in the industry. Additionally, most of the large national firms have merged with international groups or have created new international subsidiaries. Therefore, the concept of an actual Big Eight that make up the largest firms in the nation or the world may be a thing of the past.

In any event, this list is not intended to be comprehensive, nor exclusive in nature. Rather, the eight accounting and auditing firms listed below are simply some of the largest and oldest in existence.

Arthur Andersen & Co.
Coopers and Lybrand
Ernst & Whinney
Peat Marwick Main
   & Company

Arthur Young & Company
Deloitte Haskins & Sells
Touche Ross & Company
Price Waterhouse & Company

APPENDIX B

FINANCIAL ANALYSIS

It pays to know how a company is analyzed.

This appendix is designed for those who wish to learn more about the tools of financial analysis used in the business world.

How Banks Use Financial Analysis

As discussed in an earlier chapter, the process banks use to approve commercial loans often includes a trip to the loan committee. Here, the application is reviewed in an analytical manner. The financial statements that have been included with the application will be a major factor in the application's success, whether they are statements of past operating history or projections of future operations.

It can be a tremendous help if the applicant knows exactly what formulas the bank uses when it judges the merits of a company's financial statements.

Analysis by Other Users

Banks aren't the only ones who use the tools of financial analysis, of course. Potential investors, especially the more sophisticated ones, often use the same formulas to compare the companies competing for their investment dollars.

These analytical tools can help businesspeople, too, by giving them a method of comparing the performance and financial strength of their company against their competitors'. If a business can be compared to a living organism, then financial statements represent the organism's vital signs. They can be used to monitor the health of the business and to guard against potential problems.

There are seven commonly used tools for financial analysis that will be examined here: four ratios, one turnover rate, and two percentages. Each of these formulas measures a different aspect of a business, and each is important for a different reason.

To make it easier to understand just what it is that these formulas are measuring, we'll use a simple set of financial statements (see Table B–1) and actually calculate each of the ratios and percentages using the numbers on those financial statements.

For each of the ratios and percentages discussed, a calculation will be performed using the amounts in these statements.

Current Ratio

Formula: current assets / current liabilities

Example: $190,000/$95,000 = 2:1

(said "two to one")

The current ratio is one of the most commonly used ratios in financial analysis. It measures the company's ability to pay its obligations over the next year.

Recall that current assets are amounts that are convertible to cash within one year, while current liabilities are amounts that must be paid within one year. In our example company's case, its current assets of $190,000 represent a ratio of 2 to 1 (written 2:1) over its current liabilities. In other words, for every dollar of current liabilities, the company has $2 in current assets.

The size of the company and the nature of its business affect whether a particular ratio is good or bad, but in this case, a 2:1 ratio is probably fairly good. A ratio of 3:1 would be even better (reflecting even more current assets to current liabilities), while a ratio of 1:2 would be decidedly bad (twice as many current liabilities as current assets).

TABLE B—1
Sample Financial Statements

A Fiction, Inc.

Balance Sheet
December 31, 1999

Assets
Current assets:

Cash	$ 30,000
Accounts receivable	$ 70,000
Inventory	$ 90,000
Total current assets	$190,000

Property and equipment

Land	$ 30,000
Buildings	$110,000
Equipment	$ 65,000
Less accumulated depreciation	$ (25,000)
Total property and equipment	$180,000

Other assets

Patent costs	$135,000
Total assets	$505,000

Liabilities and equity

Liabilities
Current liabilities

Accounts payable	$ 50,000
Current notes payable	$ 30,000
Income taxes payable	$ 15,000
Total current liabilities	$ 95,000

Long-term liabilities

Note payable	$ 65,000
Total long-term liabilities	$ 65,000
Total liabilities	$160,000

Equity

Common stock	$100,000
Retained earnings	$245,000
Total equity	$345,000
Total liabilities and equity	$505,000

TABLE B–1—Continued

A Fiction, Inc.

Statement of Income

Sales	$400,000
Cost of goods sold	$160,000
Gross profit	$240,000
Operating expenses	
Accounting and legal costs	$ 12,000
Auto and truck expense	$ 7,000
Depreciation expense	$ 11,000
Insurance	$ 5,000
Rent	$ 24,000
Salaries and payroll taxes	$ 86,000
Supplies	$ 8,000
Other taxes	$ 6,000
Miscellaneous costs	$ 11,000
Total operating expense	$170,000
Income before income taxes	$ 70,000
Provision for income tax expense	$ 24,000
Net income	$ 46,000

How can this ratio be changed? As the company goes about its everyday business, it probably *will* change. But the company's management could change the ratio through extraordinary means: They could arrange with their local bank to refinance the $30,000 current note payable, making it a long-term debt due in two or three years. This would reduce the company's current liabilities by $30,000, dropping them to $65,000, making the current ratio 3:1 ($195,000 / $65,000). By this single action, the company's financial condition would have improved, even though it still owes the same amount of money. The difference is that the company now has a longer period over which to earn income to pay its debt.

To the fledgling entrepreneur, this sort of shuffling of finances—"debt manipulation," as it's called in the financial world—may not mean much. But it means a *lot* to bankers and investors.

Quick Ratio

Formula:
(cash + securities + receivables) / current liabilities

Example: ($30,000 + $70,000)/$95,000 = 1.05:1

The quick ratio is a much tougher test of a company's ability to repay its current liabilities than is the current ratio—so much tougher, in fact, that the ratio is often referred to as the "acid test." The ratio is called the "quick ratio" because it measures the ability of the company to repay its liabilities as quickly as possible.

To do this, the company's inventories and other slow-moving assets are excluded from the computation, leaving only cash, customer accounts-receivable, and marketable securities (such as blue chip stocks that are easily traded) to offset the company's current liabilities. In essence, the ratio shows the condition the company would be in if it were forced to cease all operations immediately and pay off any debts that were due in the next year, using only its cash or near-cash assets.

In the case of the example company, this would mean that the inventory of $90,000 that was used in calculating the current ratio would be excluded from the computation of the quick ratio. Instead of dividing the $190,000 of current assets by $95,000 (total current liabilities), as we did with the current ratio, only $100,000 in assets would be applied against the $95,000 in liabilities.

The inventory of $90,000 is excluded because no one can really be sure what the value of that inventory would be if it had to be sold in an emergency. $90,000 may have been paid for it, but in a distress sale, it might be worth only one-tenth of that amount. Perhaps, given enough time, it could be sold for what the financial statements show it is worth, but the quick ratio assumes that the company isn't going to *have* that time.

As with all the ratios, what constitutes good and bad is going to vary from industry to industry. But generally speaking, a quick ratio that is 1 or above is reasonably healthy. This shows that the company *could* cover all its next year's debts simply from its current cash or near-cash assets without having to liquidate equipment or sell inventory at distress prices.

For the example company, a ratio of 1.05:1 reflects that we have $1.05 in "quick" assets for every $1 in current liabilities.

Ratio of Stockholders' Equity to Liabilities

Formula: total stockholders' equity / total liabilities

Example: $345,000 / $160,000 = 2.16:1

The ratio of stockholders' equity to liabilities compares the book value of the stockholders' share of the company (stockholders' equity) against the total amount due to lenders or owed as other debts (total liabilities).

There are only three places from which the funds can come for a company to acquire its assets. They come either from money contributed by stockholders ("contributed capital") and from the profits of the company ("retained earnings")—either of which is part of stockholders' equity—or they come from money the company has borrowed. So the total value of the assets of the company can be divided at any time into the amount of the company's liabilities and the amount of the stockholders' equity.

The balance sheet for the example company shows that its total liabilities are $160,000 and its total stockholders' equity is $345,000, for a total of $505,000. This is the same amount as the company's total assets. These two totals will *always* be the same for *any* company. That's why the balance sheet was given its name, because the two totals are always in balance.

This company's ratio of equity to liabilities is $345,000 to $160,000, or 2.16 to 1. This means the stockholders "own" $2.16 worth of assets free and clear of any debt for each $1 worth of assets they have borrowed against.

If this company were one that had just begun its operations, this would mean the stockholders had put in $2.16 of their own money for every dollar they had borrowed. If the company had been established for a while, it would mean there was $2.16 from a combination of the stockholders' original investment and the past retained earnings of the company for each dollar the company had borrowed. For most industries, this would be considered a reasonable ratio.

Ratio of Sales to Assets

Formula: sales / total assets

Example: $400,000/$505,000 = .79:1

This ratio is used to measure the efficiency with which the company uses its assets to create sales.

Obviously, it costs money to make sales. Advertising costs must be paid, sales staff has to be paid, administrative costs must be covered, and a product or service must be produced. Of course, different types of businesses make different levels of profit on the items they sell. But if two companies sell the *same* item at the same profit per item, then the one that is able to generate the most amount of sales for the least investment is the better of the two.

In the case of the example company, the statement of income shows annual sales of $400,000. Comparing that amount to the total assets on the balance sheet of $505,000 shows that the company has generated only 79 cents in sales for every dollar of assets owned (.79 to 1). At first glance, this doesn't seem very impressive, but it would have to be compared to the performance of other businesses in the same industry to fairly evaluate its performance.

But the percentage derived for this year could always be compared against last year's performance. If only 60 cents in sales had been generated last year for every dollar in assets owned (a ratio of .6 to 1), then it would be obvious that the company's performance was improving.

Receivables Turnover

Formula:
accounts receivable balance / (1/12 annual credit sales)

Example: $70,000/$33,333 = 2.1:1

"Receivables turnover" is another measure of the efficiency with which a company is run. Of course, whether a company can calculate receivables turnover depends on whether it has any accounts receivable. A fast-food franchise store, for instance, wouldn't be very likely to accept anything other than cash from its customers.

Many businesses, though, *do* offer some form of credit to their customers, and for those who do, receivables turnover is a measure of how quickly the company *collects* on those credit sales. The length of time over which a company is owed money by its customers is often a reflection of the financial stability and strength of those customers, and that could affect the risk of debts becoming uncollectable.

As an example, a company with a ratio of .5 to 1 (meaning the company's customers pay in an average of half a month) probably stands considerably less risk of its customers failing to pay than one that has a ratio of 3 to 1 (meaning its customers take an average of three months to pay).

Another important factor is that money that is tied up in accounts receivable is money that *can't* be used somewhere else, whether the other use is for expansion or just to sit in a savings account and earn interest. Cash is an asset that should be earning a return of some sort, and cash that is owed to the company by its customers is *not* earning a return.

Gross Profit Percentage

Formula: gross profit / total sales

Example: $240,000 / $400,000 = 60%

The gross profit percentage is also referred to as the "gross margin" percentage. It measures the company's profit after only its *direct costs* have been deducted from its total sales.

A company's expenses can be divided into those that are direct and those that are indirect. Direct cost usually includes only the actual cost of merchandise that is sold or the actual cost of labor that is billed out for a service company. As an example, a law firm would consider the cost of the time spent by attorneys and para-legals actually working on specific clients to be direct costs. A retail store, however, would consider only the cost of the items it sells to be direct cost.

"Gross profit" is the difference between the amount of total sales and the direct cost of those sales. The gross profit percentage is therefore the portion of those total sales that were gross profits.

Net Profit Percentage

Formula: net profit / total sales

Example: $46,000/$400,000 = 11.5\%$

The net profit percentage is the bottom-line test of the amount of a company's profits on its sales. It includes all the expenses of the company and is the percentage of its total sales that it is able to keep as profits. This is the number that is often referred to as the "bottom-line percent."

Financial Analysis as a Management Tool

Bankers and professional investors don't just use these formulas because they are part of a time-honored tradition. They use them because they tell a great deal about the financial strength and stability of a company and about the efficiency with which it earns a profit. They also provide a clear and unbiased basis for comparison of two similar companies.

It is for precisely these reasons that the ratios and formulas should be applied to a business by the company's management on a regular basis. Doing so will give management a clear view of the current financial position of the company and the trend it is taking. The amounts used in the computations are all readily available from the standard financial statements of a business, and the computations themselves are quite simple. This is one of the simpler steps that management can take to give its company an advantage over its competition.

APPENDIX C

REFERENCE AND
RESEARCH MATERIALS
Books, Reports, and Directories

Standard & Poor's Industry Surveys

These reports are contained in several volumes and are prepared by professional analysts, economists, and researchers, each a specialist in a particular industry. Facts and figures are given for each of the major American industries, with the opinions, insights, and forecasts of Standard & Poor's experts.

D & B Million Dollar Directories

The Dun & Bradstreet Corporation publishes several directories containing information on private and public companies. Each of the directories lists companies that meet a certain set of minimum guidelines, such as net worth or sales volume.

The first few pages of each volume give a brief description of the types of companies in the volume. Companies are arranged alphabetically, but there is a cross-reference which allows you to locate companies by their industry, using either S.I.C. code (explained below) or geographic area. The main listing for each company gives the company's complete name, its address and phone number, officers and directors, approximate sales volume, a brief description of the products and services offered (along with their S.I.C. numbers), and whether the company is publicly or privately held.

240

Standard & Poor's Register of Corporations, Directors, and Executives

The information in this directory is very similar to the Dun & Bradstreet directories, and it uses a similar cross-reference system. Most libraries will have only one or the other of these two directories.

Office of Management and Budget Standard Industrial Classification Manual

This is also known as the "S.I.C. Manual." It is a hardcover directory in which most industries are given a specific "S.I.C. code," a number that makes it easier to locate similar or competitive businesses in other directories, reports, and manuals. This manual should be used to locate the four-digit code for the industry you wish to research. The number can then be used for the cross-referencing necessary to construct lists of companies in your targeted area of interest.

Dun & Bradstreet Reports

Some libraries will also have binders containing the well-known D & B Reports on selected companies. If these reports are available in your library at all, they will most likely be on a small group of select companies. They give recent financial statements and a brief credit history on each company and information on recent changes in management or control. If these reports are available, they can give you good information on some of the other companies in your industry.

Standard & Poor's Stock Reports (Public Companies Only)

These are one-page reports on many, but not all, publicly held companies. The reports are contained in a series of binders, one series for the New York Stock Exchange, one for the American Stock Exchange, and one for Over-the-Counter companies. Each report summarizes a company's recent developments, its prospects for the future, and its financial condition. If your local library doesn't have these reports, they are available at nearly any stockbrokerage firm.

Annual Reports and 10-K Reports
(Public Companies Only)

All publicly traded companies are required by the Securities and Exchange Commission (SEC) to file Annual Reports and 10-K Reports. The reports serve as management's message to shareholders and the general public about each company's performance over the prior twelve-month period. The Annual Report contains a letter from the top executive of the company explaining what has transpired over the year, a set of financial statements with an explanation of changes since the prior year, and a general section discussing the products and services the company offers.

The 10-K Report, on the other hand, dispenses with much of the flowery prose contained in the Annual Report and concentrates on specific areas mandated by the SEC: a description of the company's business, the effect of inflation on the company, the company's inventory policy, its seasonality or cyclicity, its competition, legal proceedings, assets and property holdings, and its executive compensation.

These reports—the Annual Report and the 10-K Report—can sometimes be found in the reference section of a library, but it's unlikely that you'll be able to find reports on all the companies you need there. A local stockbrokerage firm may be able to supply you with some of them, or you may have to write or phone the various companies for copies. The companies will send you their Annual and 10-K Reports free of charge, no questions asked. You should have their address and phone number from previous research sources.

Trade Magazines and Other Industry
Publications

Most major libraries have a separate section where periodicals are kept, with its own librarians who are very familiar with the contents of the section and with the various reference tools you can use to find specific items or topics. In this periodical section you will find the newsletters, magazines, and newspapers that deal with specific industries as well as all the usual general interest publications.

Almost every industry has at least one magazine or newspaper devoted exclusively to news about products, developments, personalities, and companies within that industry. These publications can provide exceptional information about the condition and direction of the industry as a whole as well as about its main participants (your potential competition).

Annual Statement Studies
Published by Robert Morris Associates, this reference work is used by lenders to obtain average financial ratios of various industries. These ratios are the basis for comparing a company's financial performance against the averages of companies within the same Standard Industrial Classification (S.I.C.).

Moody's Manuals
Moody's publishes several manuals containing historical and financial information on public companies in a wide range of industries. These manuals are updated continually, with recent information contained in a Daily News looseleaf binder accompanying each set of manuals.

APPENDIX D

SAMPLE LETTER OF INTENT (LOI)

Dear Mr. _____ :

This Letter of Intent sets forth the basic terms and conditions pursuant to which we would acquire all the issued and outstanding capital stock of _____ . The terms and conditions set forth hereunder, when agreed to by you, will provide the basis for a legally binding contract to be drafted by our attorneys. After its execution, this contract will constitute the agreement between us. This letter is not intended to be a contract, but only written evidence of our general agreement to basic terms and conditions.

1. The purchase price shall be $ ____ .
2. Costs, including professional fees, shall be the obligation of the party incurring such costs.
3. An Agreement for Purchase and Sale will be prepared, to the satisfaction of both parties, and executed prior to closing.
4. The cash to be paid to the Seller at closing shall be equal to the (audited) net worth of (Company) as of the date of closing.
5. The minimum net worth at closing shall be $ ____ .
6. Acceptable employment contracts will be negotiated with key employees.
7. The difference between the purchase price and the cash to be paid at closing shall be represented by a class of

Redeemable Preferred Stock carrying a dividend of _____ percent.

8. A cash deposit will be made by the Purchaser at the time the Agreement for Purchase and Sale is executed.

9. The Redeemable Preferred Stock will be redeemable for a ten-year period as set forth on Schedule A attached hereto. The annual amount to be redeemed shall be the amount provided in column A, or one-half (1/2) of the excess over $ _____ in pre-tax net income of (Company). Should there remain any Preferred Stock at the end of ten years it shall be redeemed in full on the tenth anniversary of the closing. The Preferred Stock shall be subordinate to bank loans.

10. The closing date will be between 60 and 90 days after the Agreement for Purchase and Sale is executed.

11. Purchaser and Seller shall conduct such due diligence procedures as are required by their respective boards of directors, and the contract shall be subject to final approval by the respective boards of directors.

If the foregoing accurately sets forth the basic terms and conditions of our proposed transaction, please execute the enclosed copy and return it to the undersigned to serve as the basis for preparation of a binding agreement.

Very truly yours,

(PURCHASER)

BY: _____

, its President

AGREED TO AND ACCEPTED BY
(SELLER)
BY: _____
, its President

APPENDIX E

THE TIME LINE OF AN IPO*

Once the two parties (issuer and underwriter) agree to go ahead with the deal, the schematic below describes the general schedule that will follow after the IPO firm (called Company below) has decided on its counsel and its printer (for documents). Once that sequence starts, the company's officers and the managing underwriter will make no statements about the proposed new issue without clearance from company counsel and underwriters' counsel.

Tentative Time Schedule for Public Offering of Common Stock

Required actions prior to public offering
Company selects counsel and printer.

Company officers, directors, and managing underwriter make no statements about the proposed public offering without prior clearance from Company counsel and underwriters' counsel.

Nine weeks prior to offering date
Company, its accountants, and counsel begin assembling required data, including financial statements and exhibits, to be included in the registration statement.

Company makes available to underwriters' counsel the Board of Directors' meeting minutes for prior years and abstracts all important contracts for review by such counsel.

Company officer and Company counsel prepare and make available the first draft of the business, property, management's discussion of earnings, competition, and employee sections of Part I of the registration statement.

First draft of underwriting agreement to be available from underwriters' counsel.

Conference with managing underwriter, underwriters' counsel, and Company officers, counsel, and accountants to discuss the time schedule and initial document drafts.

Eight weeks prior to offering date

Board of Directors authorizes preparation of the registration statement and related documents.

Accountants prepare the audited financial statements for inclusion in the registration statement.

Company counsel begins preparation of Part II of the registration statement including exhibits.

Managing underwriter and underwriters' counsel begin preparing the first draft of the remaining sections of Part I of the registration statement, agreement among underwriters, underwriting agreement, underwriters' questionnaire, and underwriters' power of attorney.

Company counsel prepares questionnaires to be sent to officers and directors as to interest in material transactions.

Seven weeks prior to offering date

Second draft of the registration statement and underwriting agreement to be available.

Tour of principal Company facilities by managing underwriter and discussions with principal management personnel of the Company to assist managing underwriter in gaining a complete understanding of the Company.

Conference with managing underwriter, underwriters' counsel, and Company officers, accountants, and counsel to discuss second draft of the registration statement and related documents. Reworked second draft and the registration statement and related documents sent to financial printer for page proof.

Six weeks prior to offering date

Managing underwriter, underwriters' counsel, and Company officials, accountants, and counsel continue to work jointly on the preparation of the registration statement and related documents.

Five weeks prior to offering date

Company counsel and underwriters' counsel jointly prepare appropriate resolutions for the Board of Directors' meeting to be held at the time of the initial filing of the registration statement.

Managing underwriter submits a list of the prospective underwriters for review by the Company.

Four weeks prior to offering date

Board of Directors (1) approves preparation, execution, and filing of the registration statement and all amendments thereto (except the price amendment) and related matters, (2) authorizes qualification under state "Blue Sky" laws, (3) authorizes Company officers to negotiate with the managing underwriter as to the terms of the offering, and (4) takes any other action necessary.

Registration statement filed with SEC and a copy of the tentative time schedule delivered to the branch chief of the SEC who will review the registration statement and related documents forming a part of the registration statement.

Preliminary prospectuses printed in quantity.

Managing underwriter issues press and "broad tape" releases relating to the filing of the registration statement.

"Blue Sky" action is initiated by underwriters' counsel on behalf of the Company to register the proposed offering with various state security commissions.

Managing underwriter forms underwriting group and mails copies of the registration statement and related documents to members of such group.

Preliminary prospectuses broadly distributed to prospective underwriters, dealers, institutional investors, and individuals.

Company orders initial quantities of stock certificates.

Three weeks prior to offering date

Company counsel and underwriters' counsel prepare appropriate resolutions for the Board of Directors' meeting to be held at the time of the determination of offering terms and the filing of the price amendment to the registration statement.

Underwriters' due-diligence meeting to discuss the registration statement with Company officers, accountants, and counsel.

Information meetings held in certain cities such as Chicago, Los Angeles, and San Francisco to acquaint underwriters and dealers with the Company and its management.

Two weeks prior to offering date

Executed underwriters' questionnaire forwarded to Company counsel.

Company counsel contacts SEC branch chief to confirm anticipated date of receipt of SEC comments on the registration statement.

Quarterly or "stub" financial statements made available, if applicable.

One week prior to offering date

Receive comments from SEC on the registration statement.

Managing underwriter, underwriters' counsel, and Company officers, accountants, and counsel correct deficiencies in the registration statement and, if necessary, file amendment no. 1 to the registration statement with SEC.

Preliminary prospectus distribution letter from managing underwriter sent to SEC along with letter requesting acceleration of the registration statement from managing underwriter and Company.

"Tombstone" advertising proofs prepared by managing underwriter for release on the day following the effective date of the registration statement.

Company and managing underwriter prepare press release and "broad tape" release relating to the effectiveness of the registration statement and the public offering terms.

Week of Offering

Managing underwriter meets with Company officers to negotiate terms of the offering.

Board of Directors (1) approves offering terms; (2) approves registration statement, including amendment no. 1 thereto, if any; ratifies actions of Company officers in executing and filing same; and authorizes Company officers to execute and file all further amendments and supplements thereto; (3) approves the form of underwriting agreement and authorizes Company officers to execute and deliver an underwriting agreement in substantially such form; (4) approves the indemnity agreement; (5) authorizes the issuance of the stock to be sold by the Company upon proper documentation; and (6) authorizes all further actions as may be necessary to give effect to and facilitate the public offering.

Managing underwriter and Company officers, accountants, and counsel prepare pricing amendment to the registration statement including the underwriting agreement and agreement among underwriters.

Offering date

Managing underwriter and Company execute the underwriting agreement.

Price amendment filed with SEC (after underwriters execute agreement among underwriters).

Company receives SEC order declaring the registration statement effective and so advises the managing underwriter.

Registration statement and the final prospectus forming a part thereof printed in quantity.

Underwriting agreement delivered to respective signators.

Underwriters' counsel transmits relevant information to "Blue Sky" authorities.

Managing underwriter commences public offering of the stock and so advises the Company.

Managing underwriter releases "tombstone" advertisement for appearance on the day following the offering date and issues press release and "broad tape" release relating to the effectiveness of the registration statement and the public offering terms.

Day after offering date

"Tombstone" advertisement appears in selected newspapers throughout the United States.

Matters to be completed prior to closing

Managing underwriter provides registrar with the names in which the certificates are to be registered.

Managing underwriter packages certificates for delivery.

Day before closing

Preliminary closing with underwriters and Company counsel.

Closing

Payment for and delivery of shares sold.

Documentation required from and by managing underwriter and Company delivered to appropriate parties.

Note: Special circumstances may require departures from the above outline, particularly as to the scheduling of Board of Directors' meetings, the period of time required to prepare audited financial statements and draft the description of business sections of the Registration Statement, and the period of time required by the SEC to review the Registration Statement subsequent to the initial filing. With regard to the SEC review of the Registration Statement, the above time schedule provides for a period of approximately four weeks from the date of initial filing to the effective date of the Registration Statement. This time period may vary depending upon the number of Registration Statements and Proxy Statements currently being processed by the SEC and certain other factors.

---

*From *Inside Investment Banking*, by Ernest Bloch.   Dow Jones-Irwin, 1986. Reprinted with permission of the author.

INDEX

DATE DUE

HIGHSMITH 45-102   PRINTED IN U.S.A.

124969